A PLUME BOOK

THERE'S A SPOUSE IN MY HOUSE

PETER SCOTT is the author of *Well Groomed: A Wedding Planner for What's-His-Name (and His Bride)*. A graduate of Harvard University, he resides in Los Angeles, where he lives in a house with his spouse.

THERE'S A SPOUSE IN MY HOUSE

A Humorous Journey Through the First Years of Marriage

Peter Scott

A PLUME BOOK

PLUME
Published by the Penguin Group
Penguin Group (USA) Inc., 375 Hudson Street, New York, New York 10014, U.S.A. • Penguin Group (Canada), 90 Eglinton Avenue East, Suite 700, Toronto, Ontario, Canada M4P 2Y3 (a division of Pearson Penguin Canada Inc.) • Penguin Books Ltd., 80 Strand, London WC2R 0RL, England • Penguin Ireland, 25 St. Stephen's Green, Dublin 2, Ireland (a division of Penguin Books Ltd.) • Penguin Group (Australia), 250 Camberwell Road, Camberwell, Victoria 3124, Australia (a division of Pearson Australia Group Pty. Ltd.) • Penguin Books India Pvt. Ltd., 11 Community Centre, Panchsheel Park, New Delhi – 110 017, India • Penguin Group (NZ), 67 Apollo Drive, Rosedale 0632, Auckland, New Zealand (a division of Pearson New Zealand Ltd.) • Penguin Books (South Africa) (Pty.) Ltd., 24 Sturdee Avenue, Rosebank, Johannesburg 2196, South Africa

Penguin Books Ltd., Registered Offices: 80 Strand, London WC2R 0RL, England

First published by Plume, a member of Penguin Group (USA) Inc.

First Printing, February 2008

10 9 8 7 6 5 4 3 2 1

LIBRARY OF CONGRESS CATALOGING-IN-PUBLICATION DATA
Scott, Peter, 1976–
There's a spouse in my house : a humorous journey through the first years of marriage / Peter Scott.
p. cm.
ISBN 978-0-452-28926-0
1. Marriage. 2. Marriage—Humor. 3. Man-woman relationships—Humor. I. Title.
HQ734.S4555 2008
306.81—dc22
2007035409

Printed in the United States of America

Set in Goudy

For my parents, Ronnie and Bill Scott,
who taught me that you can still love someone
even while disagreeing with them
about where to park the car

Acknowledgments

This book would never have gotten off the ground without the guidance, support, and hard work of my agent and friend, Jennifer Joel at ICM. Thanks also to her staff, specifically Katie Sigelman and Niki Castle, for all their help.

Allison Dickens arrived at Plume shortly after this book did, and from the moment she came on board she's been fantastic to work with. Her ideas and advice have been invaluable, and more than one humorous anecdote in this book has been inspired by her own adventures as a spouse.

Trena Keating was the one who felt that Plume would be the perfect home for this book, and I thank her for launching this project and being enthusiastic about it from day one.

And thanks as well to the dozens of other people at Plume who have been involved with this book in one way or another.

And I'm most grateful for all the support from my family, especially my wife, Emily, who's the spouse in my house.

Contents

Introduction

On the weekend my wife and I got married, we felt like we were two movie stars at the opening of our summer blockbuster. Everywhere we went, people stared, smiled, and took pictures. There were dozens of conversations about what we were wearing and who did my wife's hair. Needless to say, it was a wonderful time.

And then Monday morning rolled around.

The spotlight that had shone so brightly on our "premiere" was now shifting to a similar event that was happening somewhere else the following weekend; accountants scurried about to assess the financial damage; people in attendance confessed to one another that they "drank too much and kinda had to pee through the whole thing"; all that was left to do was wait for the DVD to come out.

Of course, my wife and I were still on cloud nine. Not only did we have a blast at our wedding, but we also had our honeymoon to look forward to, during which time we planned to:

a. sleep
b. have sex
c. go into a restlike slumber and not wake for quite a while

Naturally, we knew that in time we would slowly descend from the high we were on during the wedding and honeymoon. But since we were pretty sure that people who don't come down from this high usually need rehab, we were totally okay with that.

So, we began to settle in to our lives as a married couple. We were incredibly happy, but, like all couples, we still had real-life issues to deal with. There was the ongoing task of balancing our careers with our relationship; there were the ongoing disagreements with our parents about where we would spend the holidays; and, of course, there were the ongoing debates between the two of us over the number of throw blankets that one household actually needs (me: one; my wife: five billion).

And it was in these moments that we discovered the dirty secret about being newlyweds:

Dirty Secret about Being Newlyweds

No matter how in love you are,
getting married doesn't mean every
problem in your life instantly disappears.

When I say, "problems in your life," I'm *not* talking about a pre-existing dysfunctional relationship since, ideally, if you hated each other, you wouldn't have gotten married in the first place, unless this was 1572 and the wedding was a way to create peace between your two warring empires. (But, of course, it's not 1572, and your wedding was less about global peace and more about whether Aunt Linda was having the fish or the steak.)

Instead, I'm talking about the everyday stuff. Now, those of you who are not married may be skeptical about why this is a dirty secret. "We all have bad days!" you cry. "What's the big deal?" You are the same fools, though, who say things like, "Planning a wedding doesn't seem that complicated. How hard can a seating chart really be?"

The problem for new husbands and wives is that you have just had the greatest weekend of your entire lives. You're in love. You're ecstatically happy together. Everything in your life has fallen into place at last. So why are you suddenly having a disagreement about how much money to spend on a new pullout sofa? And, for the record, is it called a pullout sofa or a sleep sofa?

As my wife and I pondered these questions, we noticed that other newlywed friends were having similar experiences:

Us:	How's it going?
Other Newlywed Friends:	Perfect! Everything is absolutely perfect. Per-fect!
Us:	Us, too. We didn't know life could be so perfect. But we heard you were thinking of moving and are having trouble finding a place.
Other Newlywed Friends:	[*nervous*] Where did you hear that?
Us:	I think the Millers told us.
Other Newlywed Friends:	THEY WERE WRONG! EVERYTHING IS ABSOLUTELY PERFECT!

What's going on? Why are we petrified to admit that we feel anything but complete bliss during the early years of our union—as though disagreeing about where to spend Thanksgiving somehow suggests that a marriage is failing?

Naturally, such fear is complete nonsense, yet it is all too common and can lead to more serious issues in a marriage later on.

This Book to the Rescue

When Richard Nixon was forced to resign the presidency during the Watergate scandal, many people thought that he would have been better off if he had merely admitted what he had done, rather than cover it up. Of course, the popular opinion at that time also suggested that it was a good idea to drop acid and wear mustard-colored clothes, so let's not go totally bonkers for everything from 1974.

But you get the idea—it's time for the veil of secrecy to be lifted. Rather than cover up the fact that the first few years of marriage can be a wild ride, this book embraces and celebrates that reality.

Naturally, *There's a Spouse in My House* is not the first book on this topic. It is, however, the first of its kind. Most marriage books tend to fall into one of three categories:

1. Books that are overly spiritual ("When things get tough—light candles!")
2. Books that are overly inflammatory ("If you disagree on the best variety of olives—get counseling! You're doomed!")
3. Books that are overly flippant ("Of course you're fighting! You're married! Just ignore each other and try having babies to ease the pain!")

In contrast, this book is much more even-keeled. Its goal is to make you more relaxed, not more stressed out. (This book will never ask you when you're going to have children!) In truth, this can be an easy goal to accomplish because many of the issues you'll encounter during the first year of marriage don't have to become overly complicated.

The problem isn't so much the issues themselves, but rather the fact that most couples haven't been told to expect any of them. We've been programmed to think that only crazy people disagree about where to put the new lamp or whether buying a new car is the right decision. Thus, we're totally unprepared for the inevitable lighting debate that we all face, and that's what can lead to stress. (The living room, incidentally, is the only logical place for the lamp and any suggestion of putting it in the bedroom is completely ludicrous.)

In time, of course, these quirky moments will become a celebrated rite of passage. But when you're going through it all for the first time, the "we'll be laughing about this later" sentiment can turn into "Are you laughing now? Because if you're laughing now, that's really weird. This is not funny yet." And sometimes it starts to feel like the "not yet funny" moments of the marriage are vastly outweighing the bliss you were expecting. But remember: that's not actually the case. We're talking about *little* issues, and it's easy to keep them that way.

To help you out, think of this book as a road map. It describes what you can expect during your first years of marriage so that you can both bask in the glory of the many happy moments and, at the same time, avoid being blindsided by any curves in the road.

The chapters start with the issues you'll face soon after the honeymoon (such as: "Why did we decide to have the wedding band play three hours of overtime for a cost of $4,200?") and end with the topics that will still be creeping up as you celebrate anniversary after anniversary together (such as: "Um . . . is this our third or fourth anniversary? And is there really a difference?").

Once you know what's coming, I think and hope you'll be able to enjoy, laugh at, and celebrate these marriage moments when they arrive. After all, you don't ever want to lose sight of the fact that (a) you've found the partner you've always wanted and (b) you have that bitchin' new blender that you got off your wedding registry: margarita madness!

Above all else remember this: having a spouse may not make all your problems instantly disappear, but it definitely makes them easier to deal with.

For the Husband and for the Wife

At the end of each chapter, I've included separate (but still shockingly fun!) sections for both the husband and the wife in which I suggest ways that each of you can make sure that the bumps in the road of marriage never grow into potholes.

Why the need for separate sections? Men and women tend to approach problems very differently and therefore benefit from different advice. As a general rule, women like to fully understand both how a problem came about and what can be done to prevent it in the future. Men, on the other hand, just want to know if it's their fault (likely) and if they should apologize (definitely).

Naturally every couple is different, and only the two of you will know for certain which advice is relevant for your relationship. In certain couples, moreover, some of the tips for the husband may actually be more relevant for the wife and vice versa. And in some cases you may—get this!—find that advice is useful for *both* of you.

So here's to an exciting marriage together! It's going to be an adventure, and you're absolutely going to love it.

And, seriously, when are you having children?

THERE'S A SPOUSE IN MY HOUSE

1

Why Did the Photographer Only Take Pictures of the Hot Bridesmaid?

Dealing with the Aftermath of the Wedding

In virtually every Mafia movie, there's a scene that goes something like this: A guy returns home to his darkened house after a wild evening out. He has some sexy woman with him and they start undressing moments after walking through the front door. Then, suddenly, a light clicks on in the room. A mob henchman with a name like Jimmy "Crab Cakes" Andruzzi is sitting nonchalantly on the sofa and aiming a gun at the guy. Jimmy says, "Mr. Delmonico wants his money!" and then shoots the guy in the shoulder. The guy falls to the ground in pain. Jimmy says, "Next time I won't miss!" and then walks out of the apartment with the girl, who, confusingly, was in on it the whole time.

Good stuff! That is, until it happens to you.

The two of you return from your honeymoon as giddy as can be. When you walk up to the front door of your house, though, you are immediately met by your florist's henchman, Billy "White Roses" Campo, who tells you that your final payment is due for the centerpieces. He stabs the husband in the eye with a calla lily and then the wife walks out and lives with the florist. Just kidding—the wife actually goes and gets a cold compress for the husband's eye.

The good news is that the two of you won't worry that much about the flower bill because you soon realize that *every* item from the wedding has massive cost overages. For example, you had originally budgeted $500 for the wedding cake, and the final cost was

$2,700, because you apparently ordered some optional extras like "frosting."

Focusing on one particular bill isn't possible since you need to spread your hyperventilation time evenly among the various invoices.

So now what do you do?

Well, let's start with what you should *not* do. Although it will be tempting, you want to avoid exchanging unhelpful, passive-aggressive remarks with each other, like:

Husband: You were the one who wanted the videographer, which cost $2,000, by the way.

Wife: Well, it was only supposed to cost $1,500, but I had to slip him an extra $500 to destroy the footage of you puking on the best man at the end of the night. Nice work, champ.

Remember, the two of you are a team now, and you need to unite against your common foe—namely, the vendors who are trying to rip you off. If any passive-aggressive comments are to be made, they should be directed at the caterer, who's charging you for 250 dinners even though your wedding only had eighty people.

The reality is that there's actually a huge benefit from having these outstanding bills: the vendors will still return your calls. This is important, because you're still owed deliverables from most of them, such as the wedding DVD from your videographer, the photo proofs from your photographer, and the now-obsolete ceremony programs from your printer. Had you already paid them off, you could kiss your chances of getting those items good-bye.

The two of you have just stumbled upon a valuable economic lesson that you can use for the rest of your life:

Valuable Economic Lesson
That You Can Use for the Rest of Your Life

Once you pay people the money you owe them, you will never, ever hear from them again.

Had you already paid off the vendors, you'd then have to spend another three thousand dollars to hire a bounty hunter who could scour the earth looking for your photo proofs. So in not paying off the bills yet you have actually *saved money!* Huzzah!

Luckily, it will be at least another six months until you get all the deliverables you're owed. That gives you plenty of time to sell your registry gifts on eBay so that you can raise some cash and pay off your creditors. Problem solved!

The Awkward Feedback Machine

Despite the postwedding frustrations with some of the vendors, the two of you still have fabulous memories of your big day: you were filled with happy emotions, you were surrounded by all your family and friends, and you put on a much better party than that lame Wainwright-Nelson wedding.

But then, like the inevitable soy sauce stain on the new white rug, some of these magic wedding memories will get tarnished. Here's how it works: You'll be casually chatting with one of the guests who attended your wedding. Without any prompting whatsoever—you could be talking about the autumn foliage or your love of curly fries—your "friend" will start describing some aspect of your wedding that went terribly wrong. He or she will claim to be paying you a compliment when, in fact, this person is slowly destroying memories of your special day. The two of you were happily unaware that there were any problems at your wedding. Now, you're just grateful that everyone didn't die of food poisoning or start rioting when the bar ran out of champagne.

You'll also get feedback from your family. They'll be thrilled about how everything went but, amazingly, this doesn't stop them from continuing to pester you about wedding details that you disagreed on during the planning. That's right: *even though the wedding is over, your family will still nag you about it.*

It sounds like it couldn't possibly happen, but it does.

Here're some of the faux compliments you'll get:

Comments Your Friends and Family Will Make about Your Wedding That Sort of Sound Like Compliments but Are Really Not

- "I thought it was endearing when the minister horribly mispronounced the groom's name."
- "The people who could hear the toasts seemed to be enjoying them very much."
- "No one at my table cared that the food was served ice-cold."
- "The band was playing so loudly that it helped drown out Uncle Ted's screams of anguish during his kidney stone attack."
- "You really did look like a princess in that very, very expensive wedding dress. It was definitely worth spending thousands upon thousands of dollars to have exactly what you wanted, sweetie."
- "The Millers would have loved that cake . . . had we been allowed to invite them."
- "Every expense was worth it! Except maybe the flowers."

Then, just for good measure, your family will get completely sidetracked:

Comments Your Family Will Make about the Wedding That Have Nothing Whatsoever to Do with the Wedding

- "If you thought you got a good deal on the cost of the wedding cake, we were at Costco last week and they were selling veal tenderloin for $6.99 a pound."
- "Before we watch your wedding DVD, I need to spend some time updating my Netflix queue. Is *Armageddon* the one

where Morgan Freeman plays the president? Or is it *Deep Impact?* I always get those movies confused."
- "I know it was hot during your wedding weekend, but you should see the high temperature for Phoenix tomorrow. Thank God we don't live there, huh?"

The solution to the postwedding nagging is simply to realize that you and your spouse are now family. No one can tarnish your wedding memories as long as the two of you keep the happy version alive forever in your minds.

In fact, this extends way beyond wedding memories. Your spouse isn't just family—he or she is your *closest* family member, which means that from now on you two must always be on the same team. You can't take sides with anyone else in your family except each other. The old alliances are gone and it's time for a whole new game of Family Survivor.

If your parents are still giving you a guilt trip about not inviting the Millers, presenting a unified front isn't just a good solution, it's the *only* solution. So while one of you reminds your parents that the Millers didn't invite them to their son's wedding, the other can point out that Neil Miller has social anxiety disorder and hates being invited to large group events anyway.

The Others

Truth be told, there's another set of circumstances that can further complicate your own wedding memories: the weddings of all your friends.

Naturally, the marriage of your friends is in many ways a great occurrence: you're unbelievably happy for your friends, and, more significantly, you realize that your friends' parents are much more high maintenance than yours. ("Okay, my mom is a little nuts, but at least she didn't insist on being carried down the aisle Cleopatra-style like Stephanie's mom did.")

However, these additional weddings create two major hurdles:

1. They eat up free time that you could otherwise be spending together just the two of you.
2. They create a sense of panic as you wonder things like, "Oh, God, was our wedding this disorganized and lame?"

These hurdles take on many forms, and you should be on the lookout for all of them.

Hurdle 1: Wedding DVDs

You were bored to tears during Ned and Lisa's wedding, so what's more fun than reliving it frame by frame? As a bonus, you'll also get to see three hours of bride-getting-ready footage, a bunch of awkward, rambling toasts, and a dancing montage featuring people you've never met before, even though Ned and Lisa insist that you have because "you were at the wedding together!"

Ned and Lisa are no fools. They know that you'd never willingly sit down and watch their wedding video start to finish. So they rope you in with the following comment:

COMMENT PEOPLE USE TO ROPE YOU IN TO WATCHING THEIR WEDDING VIDEO

"We just want to show you one thing."

That "one thing," of course, is the video in its entirety.

The bigger problem is that when your own DVD arrives, the last thing you want to do is sit through another wedding video. So the DVD, which cost more than many feature films to make, sits unwatched for weeks.

The solution is simply to wait a few weeks. Once the memory of Ned and Lisa's hideous DVD begins to fade, you'll be ready to watch your own DVD. And the good news is that your own DVD is, of course, fabulous. In fact, it's the best thing you've ever seen. Even though you told yourselves that you wouldn't force your video upon other people, you have now changed that stance because of the following thought:

THOUGHT EVERYONE HAS ABOUT
THEIR OWN WEDDING VIDEO
"This is really a great video."

So you invite your other friends, Phil and Nancy, over to watch the video and tell them, "We just want to show you one thing." And thus the vicious cycle continues . . .

Hurdle 2: Been There, Done That

Remember senior year in high school when you were dating that junior? Graduation day rolled around, and you sincerely told her, "Nothing is going to change when I go to college." And then 3.4 seconds after you arrived on campus in the fall you forgot that person's name, ignored her phone calls, and started denying that you'd ever dated her in the first place (classy behavior on your part, by the way).

The reason you acted like this was because when you arrived at college you were instantly over high school. (By the way, the junior you were dating moped around for a week and then started dating a sophomore and completely forgot all about you.)

The same situation applies to weddings. After your own wedding is over, you want to spend your weekends running errands, cleaning the house, or thinking up ways to avoid watching other people's wedding DVDs. What you *don't* want to do is go to more weddings.

The two of you desperately want to find a weekend when you can have some downtime, but you quickly realize that weekend might be several years away. Since your friends gamely supported you during your celebration, off you go to Andy's bachelor party and Beth's bridal shower and Stu and Alice's engagement party and Todd and Liz's wedding. And that "downtime" you crave winds up being a two-hour layover at DFW airport on the way home from the Baker-O'Callahan nuptials.

And then a magical solution enters your head. What if you just didn't go to Todd and Liz's wedding in rural Maine on New Year's Eve? Sure, you'd feel bad . . . except that you really wouldn't. You could stay home, light a fire, curl up on the couch together, and watch your wedding DVD again (since it *is* the greatest wedding video of all time).

Hurdle 3: The Bad Wedding

At your wedding, everyone was genuinely happy for the two of you, because you seem like a great match (and because you ordered a plethora of pigs-in-blankets for cocktail hour).

At some point, though, you'll attend a bad wedding. Any one of a number of things could cause a wedding to go bad, including:

- Not enough booze.
- Crappy hotel rooms that somehow cost $429 a night.
- Wow—have you seen the line at the bar?
- It's July, there's no air-conditioning, and you're in Houston.
- Two hundred guests; forty-three chairs.
- Seriously, why is it so hard to get a glass of champagne around here? Are we living in Prohibition or something?

Needless to say, those sorts of weddings are incredibly awkward. And your initial reaction is to start wondering what similar flaws there were with your own wedding.

The good news, though, is that you soon decide whatever shortcomings your wedding had, it was, overall, much better than the one you just went to. So the two of you go back to your hotel room and talk dirty to each other, saying things like, "Thinking about the wide variety of appetizers at our wedding is really turning me on."

This odd behavior on your part segues nicely into the fourth and final hurdle . . .

Hurdle 4: Competition

More than any other, this problem makes husbands and wives very uncomfortable. But the reality is this: when the two of you attend other weddings (now that you've already had your own) you will turn into the most competitive, catty people in the entire world.

Every aspect of every future wedding is sorted into two categories: better than your wedding or worse than your wedding. And if a detail is clearly better than it was at your wedding, the two of you will secretly start hoping that things go wrong, such as a melting cake, a sudden thunderstorm, or, in dire situations, a completely unhappy marriage for these two jackasses who are trying to be so much better than you with their fancy, perfect wedding.

By the way, if some detail winds up being exactly the same as your wedding, that means your friends "totally copied what we did," even if the detail in question is having a white cake or serving people salmon.

Inevitably, you will feel guilty or frustrated with yourselves for acting in this childish, competitive way. But don't worry, there's a quick and easy solution: just keep in mind that there were plenty of married people at your wedding who were doing the exact same thing.

> At the end of the day, just remember that nothing—whether it's cost overages, weird comments from your parents, or an endless cycle of other weddings—can ever truly tarnish the memory of your wedding day. It was the start of your great life together, and that's all that matters. Well, that, and the fact that your wedding was like a thousand times better than the Zimmermans'.

For the Husband

Wedding budget overages provide you, the husband, with one of the first valuable lessons of marriage: don't argue about things that can't be changed.

The wedding is over. It was great. The money has already been spent, so don't make stupid, passive-aggressive remarks to your wife about how the flowers cost more than she said they would. Such comments are not helpful.

Instead, you should debate things you can control, like whether you should pay cash to the bounty hunter who's tracking down your photo proofs, or put his bill on your credit card so you can get the airline miles.

For the Wife

Ladies, it's important that you find a moment during the first six months of marriage when you can sit down with your husband and select the photos for your wedding album. It would be nice if your husband took some initiative on this project, but he won't. And truthfully, would you really trust him to pick out the best pictures? (He likely hasn't figured out that the best pictures are the ones in which you—and, secondly, your mother—look the best, regardless of how anyone else looks.)

If you don't motivate to put together the album in the first few months after the wedding, you'll never get it done. And then it will hang over your head and slowly drive you insane. Eventually, your husband will have put together the album himself because he doesn't want you to be insane. And even though that's really nice of him, the album will never live up to your expectations because he doesn't have a good eye for those sorts of things. And the sub-par album will only make you more insane.

2

So, These Hand Towels Are Merely Decorative and Never to Be Used, Right?

Adjusting to Cohabitation

These days, most couples have lived together—at least for a few months—before they get married. Not only is it more socially acceptable for an unmarried man and woman to cohabitate, but it also allows both of you to work out any kinks in the relationship while saving some money. And with that extra cash you can do some useful things like paying off your student loans (bor-ring) or buying a needless electronic device that's completely obsolete seven days after you get it.

But even if you have lived together for years, cohabitation will have some subtle changes after the wedding. Before the wedding the two of you were busy basking in the excitement of it all and returning nonregistry wedding gifts. ("Matching pogo sticks? What an interesting choice, Aunt Sarah!")

Now, after the wedding, it's time for the two of you to really settle in as roommates. Naturally, there are a plethora of perks that go with this momentous event in your life:

Cohabitation Perks for the Wife	Cohabitation Perks for the Husband
You get to live with the man you love.	You get to live with the woman you love . . . and see her naked on a semiregular basis.

You have the added security that comes from living with a big, strong man.	You get to live in this fantasy world where your wife actually thinks you're a big, strong man . . . that is, until a burglar shows up and you run and hide.
Can't reach the top shelf? Your husband can!	Looks like you can hide your porn on the top shelf and your wife will never know.
If you can't make up your mind on a decorating decision, your husband can chime in and break your mental deadlock. And if you *can* make up your mind, he'll stay out of your way and let you do your thing.	For the first time since you were living with your parents, you have window treatments, high-thread-count sheets, and furniture that actually looks nice. All of which pales in comparison to the occasional nakedness of your wife around the house.

There will, naturally, be some growing pains that come with the cohabitation situation. Annoying personal habits, in particular, will have to be addressed now that you'll be living together forever. At one point in time, before you were married, these personal habits seemed as cute as a baby bear; now they seem as scary as an adult bear that wants to eat you. And it's often difficult to find the right moment to discuss these problems because one of you thinks, "I'm sure Ted will figure out that I hate it when he burps in bed" while the other one thinks, "How psyched is Liz that she's married to the burping champion?"

One solution might be to write down three things you'd like the other person to do to keep the household running smoothly. Once you're done, you swap lists. That conversation will go something like this:

Wife: Okay, the toilet paper thing is a big problem for me. If you use up a roll, it would be great if you could put a new roll in the bathroom.

Husband: I totally understand. I'll make a big effort to fix that.

Wife: Thanks. And, ideally, put the toilet paper onto the holder. Please don't just leave it on top of the toilet, because I always knock it over and it rolls all over the floor.

Husband: Okay, that's two things from your list. Can I give you one from mine?

Wife: That's only one thing on my list.

Husband: No, it's two. Replace the roll *and* put it onto the holder.

Wife: That all falls under the toilet paper topic.

Husband: Well, then, for one of my requests, I'd like to be able to ignore your request about putting the toilet paper in the holder.

Wife: You can't use your list to cancel out my list!

Husband: Yes, I can, because that's the second request on my list—I want to be able to use my list to cancel out your list.

After a few hours of this theater of the absurd, you reach a compromise: the husband will put the toilet paper on the holder and, in exchange, the wife will stop staring at him with her death-ray vision.

Now that a deal has been hammered out, you guys soon realize that there is a large and sometimes serious problem that comes from being honest with your spouse about his or her annoying personal habits: the behavior may not change. This (ideally) doesn't happen out of spite. Rather, old habits are just hard to change. But still, you've made it clear that leaving dirty dishes in the sink overnight drives you crazy. Shouldn't your spouse be making more of an effort? What do you do to prevent this problem from spiraling out of control?

There are three solutions:

Solution 1

Pepper your conversation with subtle remarks in hopes your spouse will take a hint. (Works about 2–3 percent of the time.)

Solution 2

Give up on the subtle remarks and remind your spouse for the 127th time that you own a dishwasher. (Works about 95 percent of the time.)

Solution 3

Do nothing and assume your spouse will figure it out on his or her own. (Works about 0.00000000000432 percent of the time.)

Climate Control

Besides personal habits, another great debate will take place about the temperature at which the inside of the house should be kept.

In general, the husband wants the house to be somewhere between five and fifty degrees colder than the wife finds comfortable . . . especially at night. As a result, each of you takes turns getting up in the middle of the night to readjust the thermostat and neither of you gets any sleep.

Eventually, the freezing wife just says that the husband is wasting too much electricity by having the air conditioner turned down to fifty-one degrees. And then, come winter, the husband says the same thing about the fact that the wife has the heat turned up to eighty-six degrees. As a result, you both look forward to April and October, because they're the only months when you both sleep well.

If the temperature issue continues to be a pest, there are several options you can turn to, to remedy the problem.

Insulate the House

This helps the house maintain its temperature. So now, when the husband cranks the A/C, the house stays cool, meaning the wife is miserable for months instead of hours.

Switch Which Side of the Bed You Sleep On

After you get married, you have about one month to determine who sleeps on what side of the bed; after that, you're psychologically locked in forever. If you try to switch sides—even in a hotel room—you'll toss and turn all night and wake up with a stiff neck. So before that happens, figure out which side of your bedroom stays cooler and put the husband on that half of the bed.

Give the Wife an Extra Blanket

Simple. Easy. Saves electricity. That is, until the night when two millimeters of the extra blanket accidentally wind up on the husband's side of the bed. He wakes up in a sweat and banishes the blanket back to the living room.

Lots of Water for the Husband; a Heating Pad for the Wife

Husband has to pee all night; heating pad accidentally ignites duvet.

Go Stay with Your Parents

You'll be so happy to return to your own bed after the visit that you won't care about the temperature.

SPACED OUT

The truth is that the tension the two of you may feel from each other's annoying household habits or climate control preferences is actually a symptom of a bigger problem: space.

When you live together, you're trying to squeeze all the wife's stuff, all the husband's stuff, and all the stuff you got from the wedding into a space that's comically small. Anyone is bound to be tense when the lack of shelf space means you have to sleep on your books and shower with your framed photography.

As a result of the space crunch, not everything will get to go where you want it. To illustrate the point, here's a fun match game that shows where things will wind up.

Fun Match Game!

Match the following objects with their new destination after cohabitation starts.

Item	New Location
Wife's favorite piece of art	The town landfill
Husband's favorite piece of art, which, incidentally, is less "art" and more "Playmate wall calendar"	The wall above the fireplace
Husband's beat-up old easy chair that has springs coming out of it	In the fireplace (while fire is lit)
Husband's terrible futon	Somewhere out of sight
Husband's Coed Naked T-shirt collection, all of which are browning under the armpits	Goodwill
Husband's half-used jar of grape jelly that he bought at Costco eight years ago	A hole in the backyard

Fun game, right? Here's the answer key: item #1 goes in location #2. If you got that right, then you got 100 percent because the rest are interchangeable.

Keep the Farm Running Smoothly

Another issue couples face is space. Most first apartments or homes are on the small side, and the longer you live there together, the smaller it will seem. Given that space can be so tight, it helps to keep your home as organized as possible. Household chores will thus be incredibly important—you can't let trash pile up because the trash area is also where you store your canned goods, your fine china, and your cookbooks.

Most of us have done chores all our lives, but now that you're married and living with a spouse, these tasks take on a new meaning.

Making the Bed

Before the wedding, this chore involved pulling your comforter over the awkward tangle of crappy sheets on your bed. Now, after the wedding, it involves pulling your comforter over the awkward tangle of nice new sheets that you got as a wedding gift from Guy and Martha Callahan.

Also, folding the fitted sheet used to be an impossible task that you'd have to do all by yourself. Now the two of you can do it together. This doesn't make it any easier, mind you, but it's satisfying to see that everyone else struggles with folding the fitted sheet as much as you do.

You should try to resist the temptation to put up some kind of dry erase board on which you'll keep track of everyone's chores. You'll probably have to do this when you have children, but for now, it's nice if you can just have an understanding with each other of who will do what. Also, the husband is just going to use the dry erase board to draw outlines of his hand and head.

Doing the Dishes

This is an incredibly important chore because when you break your new china you want to be sure it's nice and clean.

Cleaning the Bathroom

A spotless, bacteria-free bathroom is critical for the long-term health of the two of you. Also, the bathroom acts as an extra closet for winter coats, luggage, and the vacuum cleaner. You don't want any of these items catching a cold, either.

Recycling Newspaper

No matter when you try to recycle today's newspaper, your spouse will not be done reading it yet. So you forget about doing it and just let the old newspapers pile up in the corner of your living room. Eventually, the pile gets so tall that it turns back into a tree.

Doing the Laundry

Husband announces that he is a modern man and offers to do wife's laundry for her. Wife is touched, but asks husband if he knows how to separate whites from darks. Husband says yes, not knowing what that means. Husband then promptly washes white T-shirts with red tablecloth.

Mopping the Kitchen Floor

Didn't do it before; not doing it now.

Chop Wood / Milk Cow / Behead Chicken

Um . . . where are you guys living, exactly?

It's important to be flexible enough that you can do each other's chores from time to time and, if necessary, switch some chores permanently.

This is especially true of chores that involve interacting with other humans—the dry cleaner, the postman, the sketchy dude who occasionally mows your lawn—because these people will immediately decide that they like one of you better than the other. Usually, it will be the wife, because the above-mentioned person will have a crush on her. You can fight this all you want, but eventually you both agree that if it takes your wife smiling at the UPS man to get your packages delivered on time, well, that's a small price to pay.

But there's one chore in particular that becomes a source of constant comedy: *shopping for groceries*. Both the husband and the wife have shopped for groceries before (or else they're entering the marriage very hungry and out of milk).

Nevertheless, there are some important differences that take place for the wife and the husband now that you're shopping for two instead of one.

Changes in the Husband's Grocery-Shopping Routine Now That He's Married

1. Apparently, on the back of most products, there's this thing called "nutritional information."
2. Husband is stunned to learn that in addition to selling strawberry ice cream, grocery stores also sell fresh strawberries . . . and, apparently, all sorts of other fruits and vegetables (who knew?).
3. Did you know that there are, like, two dozen brands of muesli?
4. There are other cleaning products on the market besides sponges. Your wife would like to buy all of these products, for a cost of $982.39.
5. Upon returning home, groceries should be put away into an area known as the pantry and/or the refrigerator—both of which are different from the countertop and/or the bag that was used to bring the groceries home.

Changes in the Wife's Grocery-Shopping Routine Now That She's Married

1. Even though there is only one extra person living in the home, you somehow need to get six times as much food. How is that mathematically possible? Don't ask, just buy.
2. The number of different mustard varieties in your fridge must never drop below five and should, optimally, be more in the ten to twelve range.

3. For years, you've walked down the frozen food aisle, staring at the hideous, processed, Day-Glo-colored "food" and wondered, "Who actually buys that?" Answer: your spouse.
4. There is a difference between bottled beer and canned beer: Bottles are for your husband and his three closest friends. Canned beer is for you and everyone else.
5. Your husband's razors are somehow thirty-seven dollars for a pack of four, but if you buy a different brand, he'll whine for days about how much his face hurts.

It's probably easiest, at first, to go shopping together. That way, you can show your spouse some of the brands and products you enjoy. And your spouse can look at you weirdly as you do that.

The Décor Makes the Man

The two of you will soon fall into a very comfortable routine doing chores around your home: one of you will take out the trash every night, and the other will pick up the seventeen pieces of trash that were dropped along the way. And before long it will be time to celebrate by upgrading the furniture in your home. And by "upgrade" I mean "get some."

For most couples, decorating the home together is a smooth process. Why? Because the wife simply makes all the decisions. The husband is not only comfortable with this, but he's also adequately prepared, having just planned a wedding "with" his wife.

Sometimes, though, you will be faced with a difficult scenario: AHD.

Accidental Husband Decoration
(AHD)

AHD occurs in three out of every five households, so do not freak out if it happens to you. AHD takes place when the husband adds to the décor of the house without really realizing it. I'm not talking about secretly rewallpapering the kitchen when the wife is at work. In addition to good taste, that would also require effort, so it never happens.

Instead, AHD tends to be more subtle . . . at least in the husband's mind. One of the husband's good friends has just returned from Munich and brought him an elaborate ceramic beer stein as a gift. The husband thinks it's such a cool gift that he puts it on the fireplace mantel so that everyone will notice it.

To the wife, this is the equivalent of putting a mustache on the *Mona Lisa*. The husband doesn't understand what the big deal is with the beer stein, and the wife calmly explains that she has forty-seven million different objections to the beer stein. For the sake of brevity, she presents only the top five reasons:

Wife's Top Five Objections to the Beer Stein on the Mantel

1. Drinking glasses are not décor. They are drinking glasses. What's next? Putting forks on the sofa and throw pillows in the dishwasher?

2. The living room was done in a French country theme. Putting a German beer stein in the room is not only out of place, but it's also politically insensitive to the complicated history between those two neighboring nations.

3. Because the beer stein is actually used for drinking beer from time to time, our living room now smells like a saloon.

4. If one was going to put a beer stein in a living room, the bookshelf is the only logical spot.

5. But we're not putting it on the bookshelf.

The husband counters with a very calm and rational argument: don't I live here too? And he doesn't say it in a confrontational way.

Instead, it's a sweet, innocent, "mommy-I-want-a-pony" request. The wife's heart absolutely melts and she immediately relents . . . for about a week.

A week later, the husband thinks about protesting, but then realizes that instead of spending all this effort worrying where the stein should go, he should spend a lot more time worrying what sort of frothy beverage should go into it. Thanks for solving the problem, you delicious, wonderful mug of beer!

The Biggest Problem of Them All

With your home fully furnished (by the wife, obviously), everything is now going along smoothly. And then, without warning, trouble will strike in the form of a houseguest. There is nothing kinder than putting up someone for the night . . . and nothing more likely to produce comments like, "Don't yell at me, he's *your* damn cousin."

Houseguests tend to fall into one of four categories, each of which produces its own set of challenges:

Category 1: Friend of the Husband

This is, by far, the most stressful category. It's one thing for the wife to put up with her husband's quirks and quite another for her to put up with his college roommate, who smells like vodka and refuses to wear pants indoors.

Moreover, it's unclear how long this dude plans on camping out in the den. Originally, he was in town for two days on vacation, but that was three and a half weeks ago. He's now receiving mail at your address and pays income tax in your state.

Eventually, the wife makes the husband kick out the college roommate. The husband tries to be an adult about it when he breaks the news, but winds up blaming the wife for everything. The college roommate then hates the wife for all eternity. This outcome is exactly what the wife wanted because now the friend will never be coming back. Mission accomplished!

Category 2: Friend of the Wife

The wife's houseguests also create problems, but for very different reasons. The wife's friend is kind, clean, and polite. She picks fresh flowers, bakes bread, and talks to animals. She's also beautiful. And therein lies the problem—she's too perfect. The wife is worried the husband's expectations will get out of whack with Ms. Fabulous around, so the solution is to quickly move the friend to a hotel (at the wife's expense, if necessary).

Category 3: Family Member

First of all, let's be honest: you have an obligation to put up any family member who needs a place to stay. The problem with family members isn't the fact that they want to stay with you, it's *when* they want to stay with you. Without fail, they will pick the single most inconvenient weekend of the decade to set up shop. An incredibly busy stretch at work, a problem with your indoor plumbing, or an impending winter blizzard—all of these circumstances will, inexplicably, encourage your family to come stay with you.

Since they're family, you can't turn them away. Instead, you do something far more subversive: you let them stay with you, but try to make their room uncomfortable enough that they won't rush back. You break the air conditioner; you use sheets that don't fit on the bed; you let live alligators roam the room. However, these tricks don't have the desired effect. Your family doesn't cut their trip short. Just the opposite. In their mind, the two of you can barely take care of yourselves. You need them. So they're not going anywhere.

Category 4: Stranger

Who is this person? How long will this person be here? Isn't it kind of weird that we let this stranger into our home? Yes, it is, but, oddly, it's less stressful than hosting a family member.

So how do you get your houseguests out? Here are some tried-and-true methods for subtly getting your friends and relatives to the front door:

- Announce that you're getting a very contagious cold. (If necessary, deprive yourself of sleep and walk around without a jacket in order to contract a serious cold.)
- Tell your guests that you're swamped with work. If the houseguests don't get the hint, tell them you both have unexpected business trips. And you have to leave immediately. Like in the next twenty minutes.

No matter how frustrated you both get from your houseguests, remember what I said in chapter 1: you're a team now! If a change needs to be made, you must present a unified front . . . even if it means huddling in your bedroom at night and formulating a strategy. Hotels exist for people on vacation. They also exist for houseguests who have been on your sofa for three months and show no signs of (a) leaving or (b) showering.

- Say that you have other guests coming. (For maximum believability, look upset when you say this.)
- Tell your guests that the two of you actually have plans to go away this coming weekend (no need to mention that you made those plans this morning). And you'd offer to have them stay at the house while you're away, but, wouldn't you know it, you've made arrangements to have the house fumigated while you're gone.

And, if all else fails:

- Calmly tell your spouse to deal with his crazy relative or friend. Because if he doesn't, he's going to have an even crazier spouse on his hands.

For the Husband

Gents, you will likely have more cohabitation traits that annoy your wife than vice versa. Why? Because you're a dude.

However, it's important to resist the temptation to find extra cohabitation faults in your wife just to make things equal. Accept it—your wife is cleaner than you are (and nicer smelling). Isn't that part of the reason you married her?

For the Wife

The right time to begin cohabitation varies with each couple: for some it's before the wedding; for others, it's after the wedding; and, for a small few, the answer is, "just as soon as my ex-girlfriend moves out."

Whenever you and your husband decide that the time is right to cohabitate, I recommend that the two of you move into a new place together. This is easier said than done in many circumstances, but there's a good reason behind it. If your husband moves into your place, all you'll remember is how clean it was before that happened. If you move into his place . . . well, come on, do you really want to subject yourself to that?

The truth is that it can be hard for both people to feel at home in a place that was originally just for one of you. Moving into a new place together makes it feel more like "our place" instead of "that place where your ex-girlfriend is still living even though you said she was leaving. Seriously—it's really weird that she's still there. I can't stress that enough."

3

Can We Just Rent a Child Actor to Spend Time with Our Parents?

The Immediate Pressure to Get Pregnant

Everyone who has had children will tell you that becoming a parent was one of the greatest moments of their life. And so, it's likely an event that the two of you are really looking forward to. But first, um, you'd like to get through the wedding ceremony.

Officiant:	I believe the mother of the bride would like to say a few words.
Mother of the Bride:	I'm so happy for you both! Now, Susan and David, we expect a grandkid by Christmas. Am I right, Joan?
Mother of the Groom:	You sure are, Debbie! Susan and David, you're not nearly as important to us as a toddler would be!
Father of the Bride:	I'd like to suggest Alice if it's a girl, after my mother!
Father of the Groom:	Girl? They're clearly having a boy!

[*A fight breaks out. Bride and groom regret decision not to elope.*]

Of course, the above conversation is hyperbole. Most parents show some restraint and don't bring up the topic of having children until minutes after the honeymoon ends. Here's how it actually plays out.

A few days after you get back from the honeymoon, the two of you will swing by your parents' house to show them pictures and wax poetic about all the beautiful sunsets you witnessed in Maui. Your parents will nod absently and stare at the ceiling, completely uninterested in your story about the active volcano that erupted next to your hotel. The minute the last photo is put away, your parents suddenly refocus and launch an all-out baby campaign that would make Washington, D.C., lobbyists recoil in fear. They tell you how much they want to be grandparents; they tell you you'll be great parents; they tell you that by the time they were your age, they already had six children (which is a curious fact since you only have two siblings).

Before the conversation spirals out of control, you attempt to tell your parents the following fact:

What You Try to Tell Your Parents about Having Kids

Don't worry—we want to be parents just as badly as you want to be grandparents! Just give us a second to catch our breath and we'll make everyone's dreams come true!

In an attempt to communicate this fact to your parents, you remind them that you are adults capable of making this decision on your own. Moreover, it would be irresponsible to have a baby before you were both ready and prepared to do so. And, frankly, your parents don't seem nearly concerned enough about that volcano that almost killed you.

To your parents' credit, they will instantly realize that the baby topic is stressing you guys out. They don't ever bring up the topic of grandchildren again until you guys are ready.

I'm just kidding.

Instead, your parents will go the creative route: they'll disguise their attempts to encourage you to have kids. It's worth noting that these disguises are usually terrible.

Ways in Which Your Parents Will Ineffectively Disguise Their Wishes for You to Immediately Have Kids

1. They give you a stroller as a Christmas present.
2. They discuss your sex life in a variety of public settings (dinner table, movie theater, Sea World) and offer tips on how you can make each other horny.
3. When you ask your parents what books they are reading, they respond with *Goodnight Moon* and *A Bear Called Paddington*.
4. They exaggerate their own medical conditions in hopes that their fictional declining health will act as an incentive. Your dad's dry skin, for instance, suddenly requires major surgery.
5. They talk about their friends' grandchildren as though they were tenured university professors: "Little Madison from across the street was over the other day and we had the most interesting discussion on princesses and hot dogs."

Eventually, you tell your parents that they need to be patient. The two of you want to spend just a little time together as an adult couple before you become parents. Your parents say they totally understand. They get up and go fetch some pretzels out of the kitchen. When they return, they ask if you've had enough time together as a married couple and are ready to have kids.

So . . . it might be time to take off the gloves. Here are some less-than-subtle lines you can use on your parents that should buy you a little time:

- "Every time you ask when we're having a baby, we're going to wait another month before we start trying."
- "We figure that if we wait until we're good and ready, we'll complain about parenting less than you did."

- "We want to wait until scientists figure out a way to remove the nagging gene from our family's DNA."
- "Isn't there something that one of our siblings is doing wrong that you can go pester them about?"

Your Friends and Neighbors (and Their Babies)

Your parents aren't the only ones who will be putting baby pressure on you. Inevitably, friends of yours will be expecting their first child and will strongly encourage you to join them in parenthood. Initially, the two of you are touched that your friends think you would be good parents. Then it occurs to you that this is the first time in years these particular friends have asked you to do anything with them. Why the sudden kinship?

In truth, these friends want you to have a baby because they know their social life is over and want someone else to be at the playground with them at 6:45 on Saturday mornings. But that's not what they'll tell you.

What Your Friends with New Babies Will Say to Encourage You to Also Have Children	What They Really Mean
Each day is more rewarding than the one before it.	Yesterday sucked.
When our child smiles, it lights up the room.	To be honest, we're so damn tired that the light in the room may have actually come from a lamp and not our child's smile. We just can't tell anymore.
We really feel like a family now.	The reason we didn't feel like a family before is because we didn't get married until we found out she was pregnant.

It's brought us closer together as a couple.	We're so freaked out right now that we're never having sex again.
We can't wait to have another one!	Okay—we lied about never having sex again.
Spending time with your own child is absolutely priceless.	That is blatantly untrue. The actual price of having a child works out to several thousand dollars a day.

Some friends, however, will not be nearly as subtle. They will ask you the most inappropriate questions at the most inappropriate times. You could be in the middle of administering CPR to someone, when a friend suddenly starts in with the baby questions.

Friend: So, you guys thinking about having kids?
You: Um, Ted, can you call 911? I think this guy's had a heart attack!
Friend: Yep, Barb and I have number two on the way. Reilly's really excited to have a baby brother.
You: Reilly's only a year old. Do you really think she can comprehend having a sibling? Also, have you called 911 yet?
Friend: You guys would totally be awesome parents.
You: [*Giving mouth-to-mouth*] Well, I'm confident that I'm more responsible than you are.

Since your friends—like your parents—don't seem to take hints very well, you have to come up with a line that will shock them into silence about when you're having a baby, such as:

- "We're going through an oral sex phase right now."
- "We want to wait and learn from our friends' hideous parenting mistakes."
- "Tonight we're just going to get drunk, have sex, and drift off to sleep. What are you and the baby doing?"

- "We thought it might be responsible to have kids once we've saved some money. But your plan of doing it when you're massively in debt sounds smart too."
- "We're totally going to have kids after we get back from our kick-ass trip to France, where we're going to have wine and unpasteurized cheese. And tuna. And we're also going to Italy."

The situation gets even more complicated when you are called in to babysit your friends' child. Your friends ask you for this huge favor so that they can have a few hours off to do something exotic like take a shower and eat a meal.

They will drop the baby off at your place. For the first hour, it's pure magic. Then, in the second hour, the baby starts to cry. It's unclear why the baby is crying, because it could be for any of the following reasons:

- Cold
- Hungry
- Tired
- Needs a new diaper
- Injured
- Is a baby
- Frustrated about current U.S. foreign policy

The two of you go into a panic and immediately try to address all these issues (your calls to the State Department about U.S. foreign policy aren't immediately returned, so you plead with the baby just to "give it more time because the wheels of diplomacy turn slowly"). Nothing seems to work.

By the third hour, you're scheduling a vasectomy, at which point your friends arrive to pick up the child. The minute the mom picks up the baby, the kid stops crying. Your friends thank you profusely and tell you that you're great babysitters. All you can think is, "Man—how horrible must their other babysitters be?"

And then, weirdly, you begin to miss the crying. It's like how people from the city can't sleep well in the countryside because it's too damn quiet. And so, hilariously, the one time your friends weren't trying to encourage you to have kids, they actually did. Go figure.

Do I Know You?

You'll also get additional baby pressure from complete strangers. Flight attendants, waiters, animals at the zoo—anyone who surmises that the two of you are a married couple will think it's perfectly acceptable to ask if and when you're having kids.

Such behavior is, of course, absurd. The decision to have children is an intimate and important topic and not something that is appropriate to discuss with total strangers. However, be careful how you respond to those queries. In an attempt to give these strangers a dose of their own medicine, you may start asking about *their* love life, assuming they'll realize that they have offended you with their questions. To your horror, the strangers seem more than happy to discuss their love life, which means you (a) have to listen to them and (b) are now forced to respond in kind. Ick.

Instead, try one of these very good excuses if you want to a wait awhile (or forever) before having kids. Sarcastic retorts work in the short run (and for that pesky flight attendant), but in the long run actions like the following will speak louder than words.

Buy a House

Buying a house is such an enormous undertaking that everyone will understand your need to put off having kids until you get settled in. However, you may need to put off having kids forever because the money you had saved for a stroller is currently being used to fix the giant hole your contractor put in your kitchen wall before he disappeared and never returned.

Warning! This tactic can backfire because some people equate buying a house with settling down and starting a family. To combat this, exclaim loudly how tiny and non-baby-friendly the house is. If necessary, leave pieces of glass and nails on the ground to reinforce the point.

Start a New Job

Upside: a new job requires your undivided attention for a few months. Downside: new coworkers need only a few hours to ask when you're having kids.

Encourage Your Siblings to Have Children

The old distraction technique: your parents won't seem to notice that you don't have kids if someone else in the family does. Plus, you guys get to be an aunt and an uncle, which lets you do all the fun parts of parenting ("Who wants ice cream?") without any of the lame parts ("Who wants to clean up this ice cream?").

Have Surgery

I'm not suggesting you rush out and get any unnecessary procedures. However, there are many surgical procedures that most of us have been planning to do when the time is right: laser eye surgery, tattoo removal, closing that open wound on your hand that's now turning blue. Well, the time has finally arrived! Each day spent recovering is a day without baby questions.

You'll soon realize that the best solution for dealing with baby pressure is to set some sort of timeline. Sure, it's completely unromantic but it can be unbelievably helpful.

A proper timeline is really two timelines:

The Real Timeline

The first part involves the two of you sitting down and working out a timeline that's good for both of you. There's no right answer or wrong answer. Maybe you feel like starting a family is priority number one now that you're married. Great! Or maybe neither of you feels ready yet. Also great! All you need to do is get on the same page.

The Timeline You Tell Your Parents About

Now you create a second timeline, and this is the one that you actually share with your parents. In this timeline, you build in extra months because your parents will stick to the timeline as though they were General George Patton. If you tell them you'll be having kids a year from now, they will show up on day 366 with a burping cloth.

The Questions Just Keep on Coming

If you do decide to have kids one day, it's worth noting that the baby questions don't suddenly stop just because you've become parents. Huh? How can there be baby questions if you already have a baby?

Well, here's an amazing thing about your parents:

AMAZING THING ABOUT YOUR PARENTS

They will continue to ask you when you're having a baby even after you've had a baby.

The nanosecond you are done cutting the umbilical cord with your first child, your parents will ask you when you're having a second one.

You now realize that as much as your parents sincerely wanted a grandkid, they were also just acting upon the next item on their life list of questions. Your parents must always have a go-to topic for every day of your life. Once a question is answered, they simply move on to the next one. Think about this for a few seconds and you'll realize it's true. During any given year of your life, your parents were obsessed with asking you:

- Where are you going to college?
- What are you majoring in?
- What career do you want to pursue?
- When are you going to date seriously?
- When are you going to get married?

- When are you going to have a child?
- When are you going to have another child?
- When are you going to go get a colonoscopy/mammogram—people over forty should have one every year!
- Why do you hyperventilate every time I'm around you?
- Why aren't you returning my phone calls?

Before you condemn your parents for having this life list of questions, remember that you'll do the same with your new child. In fact, seconds after your parents ask you when you're having another kid, you will walk over to your new baby and ask her where she wants to go to college. The baby responds by bursting into tears, which is appropriate because that's the same way you've always responded to your parents' questions. The apple doesn't fall too far from the tree, eh?

For the Husband

Husbands, it's helpful for you to take some initiative and talk to your wife about if and when you want to have kids. It's fine to have kids sooner, later, or never, as long as you're both on the same page. Once you know what the plan is, it will be a lot easier to confront the barrage of questions from your parents.

Truth be told, you should have had this baby conversation with your wife *before* you were married, but instead you had fifty-five conversations about what brand of beer you wanted to serve at the reception. Oh, well . . . better late than never. (And, for the record, your wedding had a kick-ass beer selection. Just ask the band!)

For the Wife

Ladies, you need to keep an eye on your husband during all the baby conversations because there's a really good chance he may have a total meltdown. Men have been known to start sweating profusely, eat an entire cheesecake, or toss a bucket of tennis balls against the garage door at 3:17 a.m. when baby conversations start. Why? Well, women have been peppered with baby questions since they were twelve years old. But this is a new adventure for your husband. It's not that men are disinterested in fatherhood or insensitive to your feelings. Most guys want to be dads and will be great at it. But when hours spent thinking about babies suddenly surpass hours spent thinking about meat, your husband is just going to need a moment alone to catch his breath (and, ideally, that moment should be spent with some meat).

4

When I Said I Was Allergic to Cats, Did You Think I Was Kidding?

The Pros and Cons of a Pet

There was one popular children-delaying technique I didn't mention in the last chapter: getting a pet. That's because owning a pet is more complicated than, say, starting a new job. Why? Well, you can always leave your job if you don't like it. But the minute you bring Mr. Peepers home from the cat shelter, there's no going back.

Of course, sometimes you actually inherit pets when you get married. If your spouse had a pet when he or she was single, that pet is going to be part of the marriage too. Don't ever put your spouse into an "it's me or the pet" decision, because you will lose. Handily.

When the Husband Already Owns a Pet

Single men tend to own giant dogs named "Hercules" or "Destroyer." The good news for wives is that these dogs tend to be very friendly. The bad news is that they express this friendliness by jumping on you when you're looking the other way. The issue, then, isn't so much if the dog likes the wife but whether the wife likes the dog.

The wife's spine isn't the only thing that Destroyer has destroyed. He's also made mincemeat of every piece of furniture the wife owns and, as a special bonus, he leaves a puddle of drool on her pillow each night.

The wife quickly realizes that Destroyer's actions aren't really his fault. He is, after all, named Destroyer. So off the dog goes to obedience school, which costs just about as much as a college education. But it's well worth the money, because when he returns, Destroyer is now a perfect gentleman. He's obedient and clean, and, amazingly, he does laundry. Also, Destroyer's name is now Simon.

When the Wife Already Owns a Pet

Single women tend to have very tiny dogs or cats. These pets also have very quirky names like Edith Piaf, Azure, or Sir Thomas Wiggington. Thus, when the husband is out walking the dog in the park, he has to scream, "Come here, Sir Thomas Wiggington!" in front of perfect strangers.

Oftentimes, though, it doesn't get to the park-walking stage. While husbands' pets tend to be overly friendly, wives' pets distrust the husbands from day one. And now that they're cohabitating, the animal is even more annoyed. Sir Thomas Wiggington is used to living with someone who smells like perfume. Now he's living with someone who smells like unwashed socks. And remember: dogs have a good sense of smell.

The solution is much the same as it was with Destroyer. Only this time it's the husband, not the dog, who gets sent to obedience classes. And when the husband returns he's obedient and clean, and, amazingly, he even does the laundry. He and Sir Thomas Wiggington are best friends.

When You Both Own Pets

In this case, the issue isn't whether the pets get along with you, but rather how they get along with each other. Cohabitation usually isn't a problem if the wife owns a poodle and the husband owns, say, a goldfish.

Sometimes your two pets can be friends. This is usually the case with two smart pets who realize instantly that they can team up against the two of you in order to get more food. You're so happy that the pets are getting along that you gladly cook them each a filet mignon each night, while the two of you dine on kibble.

Sometimes, though, there's a personality conflict between the pets.

Different Types of Pet Conflict

- Dog vs. cat
- Bird vs. cat
- Hamster vs. hungry German shepherd
- Two hungry German shepherds
- Jewish dog vs. Muslim cat

When these pet conflicts arise, one solution is to simply get out of the way and let the animals work it out themselves. Although, in the case of Jewish dog vs. Muslim cat, you should be aware that it's a complex conflict that goes back generations.

Another solution is to try to keep the animals separated. But in the case of hamster vs. hungry German shepherd, the German shepherd will simply wait until you are asleep before arranging a rendezvous with the hamster.

The best solution is to unite the two pets against a third pet. Borrow your neighbor's golden retriever (who gets along with everyone) and give him lots of love and affection. Three days later, the cat and the basset hound will come to you with a written compromise: they'll seek counseling if the retriever hits the highway.

When You Are Both Petless

If neither one of you owns a pet when you get married, then you must decide whether you'll get one as a couple. The simple truth is that pets aren't for everyone. Yes, they're lovable and cute, but that's only half the story.

Ultimately, many couples do decide to get a pet, because their life is peaceful and perfect, and that feels strange. A pet should remedy that at once.

Reasons to Get a Pet	Reasons Not to Get a Pet
Companionship.	Didn't you just get married? Don't you already have a companion who, as a bonus, sits upright and knows how to go to the bathroom in the house?
When you come back from a vacation, there's someone in the house to greet you.	No, there isn't. The dog had to go to doggie overnight camp while you were away (at a cost of $85 per day).
It teaches you how to be responsible.	After you kill three goldfish in five weeks, you'll be in therapy for years.
Your friends all seem to have one.	Every time you go to your friend's house, you return home covered in animal hair and sneezing. Why exactly would you want to duplicate that in your own home?
Protection.	Since you're both scared of guard dogs, you get a miniature white poodle. How deadly.

So Many Flavors to Choose From

Most people tend to get a cat or a dog, because these animals cause the most problems with allergies. But there is a wide range of other animals out there for you to choose from:

- *Birds*. Most birds don't carry deadly diseases, although a few of them do. But there's no reason to worry, unless you actually come in contact with the bird.
- *Hamsters*. Did you know that hamsters are nocturnal? Well, you will . . .
- *Fish*. Fish are a good low-maintenance option—you only have to spend about two minutes feeding them each day,

and the rest of the time it's like they're not even there. On the downside, if you become emotionally attached to a fish, that's, um, really weird, and probably won't end well.

- *Rabbits*. Rabbits are cute and fuzzy, but they don't really seem to like humans. They're either (a) running away from us in horror or (b) spending their time plotting a Stephen King–esque revenge on our species.
- *Snakes*. This is a terrible idea. Seriously.

Because most people have seen the movie *Anaconda*, they opt not to go with an exotic pet that may eat them, and, instead, get the requisite cat or dog.

But the choice between cat and dog is not a simple one. The decision goes beyond which pet you'd like to have. It's really a part of your overall persona. Are you cat people or are you dog people? It's like deciding whether you're city folk or country folk, carnivores or vegetarians, people who talk loudly on their cell phones in restaurants or people who want to kill those jackasses.

Beyond that, there's a zillion different varieties of dogs and cats. People who own poodles are different from people who own Dobermans. Meanwhile, witches own black cats and Bond villains own white cats. It's a hard choice!

Therefore, before you make up your mind, it's best to do a little research. You both quickly agree to visit some different venues where you can spend time with cats and dogs in hopes of finding an answer.

First, you head to the pet shop at the mall. This proves to be an unmitigated disaster. Every animal there looks sad and trapped. But you aren't able to rescue any of them because there are 3,529 kids in the store banging on the window, trying to wake up the sleeping puppies. You both fall into deep depression and head immediately to Starbucks for a rejuvenating coffee and pastry.

The next stop is a breeder. The animals at the breeder seem much happier and healthier than those at the pet shop. Unfortunately, you quickly discover that you can't actually have any of these pets. Why? Well, the breeder won't sell you a puppy because you didn't know that the Yorkshire terrier is different from the Scottish terrier. Also, you're not crazy people who live in a giant house full of dogs, so the breeder can't relate to you.

The final stop is the animal shelter. This is the most humane thing to do, anyway. And, as you hoped, your choice is made for you. Moments after walking into the shelter, an adorable little mutt gives you the puppy dog eyes (since she is, after all, a puppy) and both of your hearts instantly melt. It turns out you're dog people.

You rush home to join the American Kennel Club, who won't accept you because your dog is a mutt.

The Transition

The dog you were able to rescue now has a wonderful life in your home. And the two of you have a new companion. But it can take weeks and months for your dog to feel comfortable in its new home. This happens for many reasons:

- *New name*. You decided to name the dog Linda, because dogs with overly human names make you laugh. However, Linda doesn't have the same clever wit that you guys do. Her previous name was Skip (because her owners thought she was a boy). She was confused when people called her Skip; now she's *really* confused that people are calling her Linda. This isn't the dog's fault, though. If everyone started calling you Rover, you'd also stare at them curiously and then chew the furniture.
- *New home*. Yes, your home is (hopefully) nicer than the shelter where you got Linda. But Linda was used to the shelter. Now she has to get used to your home. She may not yet appreciate how lucky she is to live in a place that has a

handcrafted rug from Turkey. Or maybe she does, and in Linda's culture, one shows appreciation for something by peeing on it.

- *New owners.* Because you got Linda from a shelter, the odds are high that her previous owners weren't all that great. At best they were just disinterested and at worst they were abusive. Either way, Linda has become a little distrusting of people. If she could, she'd go live on her own somewhere in Montana, where she could ride horses and open a craft shop. But since she can't, it's going to take her a little time to realize that she can trust the two of you. So don't be offended when you offer her a piece of turkey, and she decides to have her attorneys look over the meat before she eats it.

Although this transition period is perfectly normal, it takes a toll on the two of you. You get frustrated at Linda from time to time, but you also get frustrated at yourselves. You become convinced you're doing something wrong, and in your panic, you say: "We're going to make terrible parents."

Ah! There it is! The revelation!

You may have gotten a pet to delay having children, but, in fact, it now feels like just the opposite. Owning a pet suddenly makes you feel like you have children. And, even worse, you think you're doing it badly.

This is a difficult moment for many couples. You're filled with the best intentions but loads of self-doubt. Maybe you two should be the ones who move to Montana and open up a craft shop.

The good news is that there's really nothing to worry about. Linda will adjust to her new environment in due time. And she already loves you for giving her food and shelter. Besides, you may not realize that you're actually learning some valuable parenting lessons that will come in handy down the road when you do have children.

Things Dogs Do That Your Children Will Also Do

1. The dog doesn't listen to anything you say.
2. The dog doesn't eat vegetables.
3. Sometimes the dog goes out and doesn't tell you where she's going.
4. The dog gets totally embarrassed when she's talking to her friends and you show up and make her come home right now.
5. The dog wants to have sex all the time and you prefer not to think about that.
6. The dog doesn't like to be held by your creepy friend Ray.
7. There is no way the dog is wearing that hideous sweater your aunt Martha made her for Christmas.

And, the most significant thing your dog will teach you about having a child:

8. Caring for another living being is a twenty-four-hour-a-day job. And most of that job involves arguing about who's going to clean up that living being's poop.

Now We're Those People

After the transitional period with your new pet ends, the pendulum will begin to swing dramatically in the other direction. You will fall madly in love with the pet and vice versa. Your feelings of self-doubt will be replaced with arrogance. Before, you thought you'd be terrible parents because you couldn't even take care of a dog. Now that the dog loves you, you're convinced that you're the two greatest role models on Earth.

Caring for Linda suddenly makes the mundane aspects of your life exciting again.

Mundane Activity in Your Life	But Now, with a Dog . . .	Although, for the Record . . .
Shopping for groceries	You spend an eternity poring over the different flavors of canned dog food, wondering whether Linda would be in the mood for beef tonight, since she had poultry last night.	Linda will eat anything. It's sweet that you care so much, but she'd happily eat the can if you served it to her.
Driving around town	You get to watch Linda stick her face out the window and smile with euphoria as her nose fills with scents.	Don't try this yourself. Just trust me.
Walking outside to get the morning paper	This event turns into a morning constitutional with Linda.	By "morning constitutional" I mean "watching Linda poop."
Coming home from dinner and a movie	Linda runs around excitedly, as though seeing you guys is the greatest moment any creature could hope for.	She's mostly excited about that doggie bag in your hand, since she is, after all, a doggie.

Linda has brought joy and excitement to your life and things couldn't be better. And then, like generations of people before you, you go a little insane with your love of Linda and slowly detach from reality. You've seen this happen with other people and laughed at them. But now, suddenly, you are those people. Have you ever:

- Talked to Linda about serious topics as though she were a trusted confidant, even though her response is almost always, "Ruff"?
- Sent out a Christmas card featuring a picture of the three of you with a caption that reads, "Happy Holidays—Gabe, Lisa, and Linda"? To a perfect stranger, it's unclear which name belongs to the dog and which names belong to the humans.
- Asked a guest not to put his or her feet on the sofa, but then, when Linda rubs her butt into the cushions, you smile and say nothing?
- Spent $25 on a sweater for yourself and $250 on a sweater for Linda?
- Tried to make dinner plans with friends and said something to the effect of, "Hmmm . . . that night won't work for Linda"?

If you suffer from any of these symptoms, it's okay. Don't get me wrong: you *are* going insane. But the journey to crazy town is one that the two of you are taking together. And that's what marriage is all about!

> I've spent most of this chapter talking about getting a dog. And I know what you're thinking . . . no love for the cat, eh? Well, the fact of the matter is that getting a cat doesn't actually change your life that much because, unlike a dog, a cat refuses to acknowledge your existence (especially if you're the husband). Although that does sound like good practice for having a teenager . . .

For the Husband

If your wife brings a small, effeminate dog with her to the marriage, don't be too macho to show some affection. Yes, these dogs tend to be a bit more antisocial than Labrador retrievers. But if you show some love, you'll get some love.

Oh, and if you're worried that it's not manly to fall in love with a tiny, effeminate dog—get over it. Now that you have high-thread-count sheets and window treatments in your home, your manly days are behind you. So there's nothing wrong with developing a deep love for a tiny dog.

Your friends may make fun of you, but your wife won't—and she's the one you're trying to impress. Besides, your friends are shallow fools who will never understand the happiness that comes from your meaningful friendship with Sir Thomas Wiggington.

For the Wife

If your husband's dog is driving you crazy, don't assume your husband is aware of this. His love of Destroyer runs deep, and it's hard for him to comprehend that there are people who don't like being covered in dog saliva.

By now, you've probably realized that your husband, while a great man, isn't always skilled at reading your thoughts. For example, there was the time you pointed out a handbag you liked, assuming your husband would get it for you for your birthday. Instead, he got you a membership to the Bacon of the Month Club.

5

Are There Carbs in Bread?

The Challenge of Staying In Shape after the Wedding

Every bride and groom in the history of civilization has gained weight after their wedding day. It is only a matter of time until archaeologists unearth a married caveman who's wearing a pair of old tux pants that were so tight he couldn't get the zipper closed.

Why does this weight gain happen? There are vastly different reasons for men and women.

Brides tend to get very stressed out in the weeks before their wedding for a variety of reasons (read: their mother). As a result of all this stress and running around, brides forget to do normal stuff like eat food and breathe air. With the wedding over, things can slowly return to normal (i.e., her mother goes home).

Men, on the other hand, have totally lost all desire to stay in shape. The only reason they were in shape in the first place was so that a woman would have sex with them. Now that they have accomplished that vital goal, it's time for burritos. With cheese. Every day.

Other non-gender-specific factors contribute as well:

Reasons for Postwedding Weight Gain

1. The two of you are no longer sweating off seven thousand calories a day in perusing your wedding guest list

and figuring out how to fit 250 guests into a chapel that holds 35.

2. "Dear Uncle Charlie: Thank you for the lifetime supply of pork sausage. It's really a fascinating wedding present. Fondly, Bride and Groom. P.S. We hope your bypass went well."
3. Since neither of you has had a productive day of work in the year preceding the wedding, your bosses get even by requiring you to work every weekend for the next twelve years. So much for an active lifestyle.
4. The twenty-seven cases of beer left over from the wedding expire in six months. Since you're "thinking globally," you decide to "act locally" by making sure no beer goes to waste.
5. Your actual wedding day was so hectic that neither of you really had time to eat. Therefore, at every subsequent wedding you attend, you make up for it by parking yourself in front of the Peking duck station.

The moment when it all hits home occurs when the photos from the wedding arrive. You'll recall from chapter 1 that this tends to be several months, years, or epochs after the wedding. But when they do show up, the people in them bear little resemblance to the two of you. The groom in the photos, for instance, seems to have only one chin, while the man looking at the photos now has at least three. "That's it!" he announces. "I'm getting back in shape . . . just as soon as I get back from Cold Stone Creamery."

Spending Money to Feel Better

Once the photos arrive, the two of you decide to get some more exercise. The first step will be joining a gym. A lot of people resist joining a gym because of the cost. But those people have yet to realize that spending the money on gym membership gives you a great feeling of accomplishment. You can proudly announce to your friends that you've joined a gym. They won't know that you've never been to the gym and don't even know how to get there. Indeed, you can go another three to six months without ever working out simply because paying gym dues is such an impressive and satisfying first step.

Once the mere possession of a gym membership no longer feels sufficient, there are, of course, many athletic activities that the two of you can pursue outside of the gym. These activities (a) allow you to feel less cooped up, (b) ensure that your gym membership dues go to waste, and (c) bring you together as a couple. And by "bring you together" I mean "the wife realizes just how damn lazy her husband really is."

Jogging

Many people prefer jogging to using the treadmill because it allows them to get outside and breathe the air. The outside, however, also has things like snow, rabid dogs, and no TV on which you can watch *Jeopardy!*/*Oprah*/anything-in-the-entire-world-to-take-my mind-off-the-fact-that-I'm-jogging.

Tennis

The sophisticated sport . . . until your friends beat you in doubles and you take them off the holiday card list. Forever.

> The one thing you don't want to do is pick an activity that will lead to excessive competition between the two of you. Playing each other in a game of squash every Saturday is great, unless the loser throws a hissy fit for the next six days. If you find that you're becoming overly competitive, try an activity that is more about well-being than competition, such as yoga. And when you somehow make stretching competitive, perhaps it's best if you take a break from working out together.

Skiing

This will be really easy to do on your way home from your office in downtown Dallas.

Golf

You drive around in a minicart all day and stop for a cheeseburger halfway through. How exactly does this sport help you get in shape?

White-Water Kayaking

Are you crazy?

Home Is Where the Gym Is

If these activities aren't your cup of tea (seriously—kayaking? Are you crazy?) and the high cost of a gym membership is getting you down, the two of you will soon realize there is another solution: the home gym.

To create a home gym, you'll first need to find an empty room in your home. Since you have no empty rooms, you'll announce that the gym will conveniently be part of another room, like the dining room or the hall closet. You only have enough money to buy one cardiovascular machine, so you opt for the elliptical machine, because people look really silly when they're using it, so you'll be able to laugh at each other constantly.

You squeeze the elliptical machine into the dining room, managing to break only a few pieces of wedding china in the process. Since one machine doesn't really make a gym, you decide to add a stretching mat (read: a towel), some weights (read: canned goods), and a water cooler (read: leaking roof in the dining room). You also want to add a TV, which, due to a lack of space, needs to sit on the dining room table. With the dining room table now a media center you'll never be able to have anyone over for dinner, but by now you don't care because you've broken the new china.

The elliptical machine is a roaring success for the first five days. Then something goes wrong with the TV picture. All workouts grind to a screeching halt until the picture can be fixed. It takes you three weeks to find the problem, which, it turns out, is a loose cable on the back of the TV. The reason the cable is loose is that it isn't really long enough to stretch into the dining room, which is also why the TV is positioned dangerously close to the edge of the dining room table.

You could solve this problem by buying a longer cable (cost: seven dollars), but that would require a twelve-minute errand, so it never gets done. Instead, you find a stool on which to balance the TV. Nine seconds into your next workout, the TV falls off the stool and breaks. With no TV, you immediately sell the elliptical machine and use the money to buy a gym membership.

Exercise is only part of the equation. You both soon realize that you'll have to eat healthier if you want to stay in shape.

If you're like most people, you'll go on approximately 3,492 diets over the course of your marriage, each one of which is brought on by a different reason, including:

- Upcoming warm-weather vacation
- High school reunion
- Realizing that the coworker in the office who you thought was your age is actually fifteen years older than you and is in much better shape
- Your wife tells you to

Sometimes the two of you will be on a diet at the same time, but more often than not, one of you will be trying the South Beach Diet while the other is trying the eat-all-the-bread-and-pasta-in-the-world diet.

The issue, of course, is that the spouse who's dieting might get a little cranky. So the onus is on the other spouse to be supportive (and eat his/her plate of linguini in private). Here's what you can do to help:

Tips for When Your Spouse Is on a Diet

1. If your husband seems moody, remember that he's not upset with you, he's upset because he had two almonds and a celery stick for lunch.
2. Be supportive if your wife is feeling down because she had a snack attack. Remind her that even though she ate a bag of potato chips, it's still healthier than the nachos you had for lunch.
3. Try and help out when you go grocery shopping. If your husband is laying off the sweets but has a soft spot for licorice, don't come home with a three-pound bag of Twizzlers (even if it's on sale).
4. Lead by example. Even if you don't feel like you need to diet, consider joining your spouse, at least at home. She'll appreciate the love and support, and, as a bonus, you now have carte blanche to be cranky about stuff too!

THE CYCLE

Once the two of you get back on the fitness bandwagon, there's a tendency to go totally insane. You hire a nutritionist. You get matching sweat suits. You measure your body fat after every glass of water. You even start hanging out with your really athletic friends Bobby and Terry (never sure which one is the wife and which one is the husband).

And then, without warning, the fitness pendulum swings back the other way. One of you sprains an ankle and the other one decides the nutritionist is a rip-off ("Two hundred dollars for this bozo to tell me to eat fish!"). You both swear off fitness forever. Not only do you never see Bobby and Terry again (assholes), but they receive the blame for everything that's wrong in your life.

Wife: We're out of toothpaste.
Husband: If I hadn't gone mountain biking with Bobby (or was it Terry?) last week I could have gotten you some.
Wife: I hope Bobby and Terry have cavities.
Husband: They do, sweetheart. They do.

This on-again/off-again fitness cycle continues in six-month intervals until the end of time.

For the Husband

As a husband, it's important for you to try to stay in shape. Your wife will already feel the pressure to do this from, um, all of society (women get a raw deal on this topic). So, frankly, guys should get a little pressure, too. You don't have to turn into Jack La Lanne, but be smart. Don't have french fries every day. You've just married the person you want to spend the rest of your life with, so take care of yourself to make sure it's a long life.

Still not convinced? Well, maybe the following equation will help you change your mind:

Smell of garlic fries + you = no sex.

For the Wife

Wives, if you're worried that your husband's idea of exercise is sweating after he eats a porterhouse steak, why not try to encourage him to work out with you? Exercising together is a nice way to make it seem less like a chore . . . and more like a competition. Just kidding. Sort of.

Whether it's jogging together, playing tennis with each other, or simply going to the gym in the same car, it's a nice way to spend a few extra waking moments with your spouse every day. Remember: the hilarity of your gym membership is best shared with someone you love. I'm referring, of course, to your best friend, Jenny, who thankfully has a membership at the same gym. But if Jenny's not available, your husband is okay, too.

6

Have We Decided Where We'll Be Having Thanksgiving in 2047?

Divvying Up the Holidays among Your Families

After World War II ended, the British, Americans, and Russians decided to divide the German city of Berlin into pieces because they thought this would be a fair way to preserve the postwar peace. Then the Cold War started and everyone spent the next forty years waiting for armed conflict to break out in Berlin.

Why the history lesson? Well, now that you're married, the holiday calendar will start to look a lot like Berlin. You'll divide each holiday into pieces and then spend the next forty years waiting for your families to go to war with each other over who gets to be with you on Flag Day. Here's a rundown of the major holidays that your parents will fight over and tips to manage each one. Let's go through the year chronologically:

New Year's Day

When you announce that you want to spend New Year's Eve with your spouse, maybe alone at a romantic restaurant, your parents will remind you that for years you always spent New Year's with them. You should remind them that for years you sucked your thumb and had an unhealthy attachment to a quilted blanket. Progress is good!

Martin Luther King Day

When your parents ask if you want to go ice fishing with them that weekend, stage a peaceful protest march.

Presidents' Day Weekend

You will wind up visiting whichever set of parents lives in a city that's having a blizzard that weekend. Best solution: pack warm clothes and entertain each other by wagering on how long your flight home will be delayed due to weather.

St. Patrick's Day

St. Patrick's Day is to be spent drunk with whichever family is more Irish. Just be sure that the spouse from the less-Irish family has been warned about what they're in for.

Easter

Even though you're in your thirties, your parents will insist on having a candy and egg hunt around the house. Aren't you looking forward to finding chocolate eggs that have been hidden for twenty years (and are now covered in larvae)? Don't eat anything you find.

Memorial Day

Even though you have flown, driven, or biked in specially to spend time with your family this weekend, your parents spend the whole time on the Internet trying to figure out the difference between Memorial Day and Veterans Day. Thus, Memorial Day weekend becomes a great opportunity to catch up on sleeping, reading, and snacking. It's your favorite trip home all year!

Fourth of July

Whichever parents you don't visit this weekend will challenge your patriotism. Send them red, white, and blue socks as a consolation present.

August

No holidays this month! God bless you, August! Warning: This is the most popular month for family vacations, though, so don't let down your guard too much. See chapter 12 for a primer on surviving the family vacation.

Labor Day

On Presidents' Day weekend you visited your relatives in Chicago during a blizzard. On Labor Day, you must now visit your relatives in North Carolina during a tropical storm. Whoever lost the plane-delay bet back in February now has a chance at redemption.

Note: Only allowable topic of conversation during Labor Day weekend is talking about how quickly the summer went by. Don't try to resist. Just bring some note cards with talking points on this subject, such as:

- "It feels like Memorial Day was just last week!"
- "I can already feel a chill in the air!"
- "We need to move to Florida, right?"
- "Let's pray for an Indian summer!"

And, the one line that someone *always* says, even though it stopped being funny (and started becoming terrifying) thirty years ago:

- "Where's that global warming I keep hearing so much about?"

Halloween

Whichever parents you didn't visit on Easter should get to spend Halloween with you, under the logic that both holidays involve candy. Keep chocolate in your mouth at all times if you want to avoid conversation (although if you get a stomachache, be prepared for a round of "I told you so!").

Veterans Day

Veterans Day should be spent with whichever family you didn't see on Memorial Day. They spend the whole day on the Internet trying to figure out the difference between Memorial Day and Veterans Day (see Memorial Day for why this is wonderful).

Thanksgiving

This is a holiday where Americans take time out from their busy lives to appreciate how much they have to be thankful for. Or, in your parents' case, to let you know that they'd be more thankful if you were spending Thanksgiving with them and not "that other family." Solution: remind everyone that fighting goes against the spirit of the holiday. And when that doesn't work, schedule a second turkey dinner for Friday night.

Christmas

The year ends with the biggest battle of them all! Whether or not either of your families is even Christian is completely irrelevant. The bride's family could be Buddhist and the groom's family could be Jewish and, amazingly, both sides will want you to come sing "O Holy Night!" with them on December twenty-fifth. Since no one will accept that you're suddenly an atheist ("What does that have to do with Christmas?!"), the best thing you can do is dust off the red sweaters and make a beeline for the eggnog.

These major holidays are merely the tip of the iceberg. Minor holidays—most of which neither of you has ever heard of before—that will also become battlegrounds:

Thomas Jefferson's Birthday

Because the husband's parents didn't get to see you over Presidents' Day weekend, they have made up this new holiday and demand that you come to the lake house with them. When the bride's family gets wind of this, they spring into action and announce that they'll also be observing this holiday, complete with a staged reading of the Declaration of Independence. Silver lining: you'll brush up on your social studies.

Your Parents' Thirty-fourth Wedding Anniversary

Next year, for their thirty-fifth anniversary, your parents are planning a big party—fun! This year, they are planning . . . absolutely nothing. But you still have to go. At least you and your siblings can bond over your parents' craziness.

Uruguayan Independence Day

No one in either of your families is Uruguayan. In fact, none of you is even sure if Uruguay is independent. But you'll be waving flags and singing the Uruguayan national anthem nonetheless. The good news: you'll be inspired to take a vacation to South America (just as soon as you have a weekend when you're not visiting your parents).

Leap Year

Four years ago, you went home to visit your parents at the end of February because you had just gotten out of a horrible relationship and needed to sulk. Now, in your parents' mind, it's a tradition! Oh, well . . . maybe they'll make you hot chocolate and tell you you're special.

Tools of the Trade

Now that you know when your parents will want to see you, it's just as important to understand *how* they will go about it. To be sure, every set of parents has its own strategy for scheduling time with you ("Mom, when did you get a job at my neighborhood Starbucks?"), but there are some tried-and-true tactics that your families will definitely use at some point. Remember: forewarned is forearmed.

Tactic 1: Guilt

The trick is to be able to recognize when your parents are using guilt as a motivator so that you can effectively call their bluff. If you're not sure what I mean, here's a handy exercise for practice.

Spot the Guilt Trip!

Circle the "guilt trip" clause in the following conversation with your dad.

You:	Well, we're off to my in-laws' house in Seattle for Christmas. Did you and Mom get the package we sent you?
Your Dad:	We sure did! A case of red wine—that's overly generous. It may take Mom and me awhile to get through it, though, since we'll be all by ourselves this Christmas because you insist on spending the holidays with that family you married into. But, seriously, you go have fun. We'll try to have fun here without you. But I doubt we will. Seriously, though, happy holidays.

The average reader, of course, can spot the guilt trip clause fairly easily (hint: it's in the part where the dad starts talking about Christmas). But when it's *your* dad talking, the guilt trip is almost impossible to spot. Instead, you hang up the phone and tell your spouse that you just realized how lonely your parents are during the holidays and maybe the two of you should carve out some time for them. Your spouse would respond, but he or she is already on the plane to Seattle without you.

Tactic 2: Bribery

It's insulting to suggest that money determines where you'll go . . . except, of course, that it's usually true. The bribes we're talking about in this case aren't cash gifts (unless your dad is Al Capone), but rather a series of small incentives that will be thrown in to entice your presence at a certain event. However, you need to be careful because there are often strings attached.

Event	Incentive Your Parents Dangle in Hopes You'll Attend	What Your Parents Fail to Mention
Family reunion at a hotel in the Adirondacks	Grandpa Sam is paying for everyone's lodging.	To save money, Grandpa Sam is sleeping on a cot in your room.
Super Bowl Sunday	Mom is making your favorite chili.	The TV is broken. Can you climb on the roof and fix the satellite dish?
Halloween	Dad's got a great costume that he's going to wear as he hands out candy.	Dad eats all the candy himself by 4:42 p.m. and figures there's no reason to dress up.
Ski trip over long Martin Luther King Day weekend	They will rent all the necessary equipment for you.	You must participate in world's most competitive game of Trivial Pursuit each evening in the ski condo.
Dad's sixty-fifth birthday trip to Portugal	Dad will pay the cost of getting everyone there.	You are traveling there by sailboat, or, as your dad calls it, "Vasco da Gama–style!"

Tactic 3: Ransom

Yes, your parents do resort to borderline illegal activity now and then to get to visit on a holiday. Ransom is easy to spot, because it's fairly straightforward. For example, let's say, for some unknown reason, you still get mail at your parents' house, even though you haven't lived there for fifteen years. Normally, your parents just put all the mail in a manila envelope and send it on to you. But now, they make you promise to spend Thanksgiving with them before they'll send you your mail.

You tell them it's a federal offense to keep your mail. They say they don't care. So, you agree to spend Thanksgiving with them . . . in Leavenworth federal penitentiary.

Tactic 4: Sibling Pressure

This is a dirty trick and your parents know it. They don't like going this route . . . but they will if they have to. Your siblings will call and have what seems like a perfectly normal conversation with you about movies, the weather, or Uncle Melvin's toupee. And then, suddenly and shockingly, your siblings reveal themselves to be pod people:

Sibling: Are you coming home for Christmas?
You: I'm not sure.
Sibling: You really should come. It's so wonderful here.
You: Yeah, well, we're really getting pulled in a lot of different directions this holiday season.
Sibling: Let me take away your fear.
You: Huh?
Sibling: Join us or perish!

You hang up the phone, realizing at once that your parents have brainwashed your siblings and sent them to do their dirty work. You don't know how your parents did this, but it probably involved complex psychological manipulation. Or maybe just money.

There's also an alternative situation, in which your parents simply use a reality check to get your sibling to exert peer pressure:

Sibling: If you leave me alone with Mom and Dad over the holidays I will freak out and never forgive you.

Tactic 5: They Come to You

If you don't make time to see your parents, they will eventually come to you. Often this happens unannounced, at the worst possible moment, like when you're throwing a dinner party and in the middle of telling a story about how your parents drop in at all hours of the day.

Naturally, it's great to have your parents come and visit. Not only have they done all the traveling (so you don't have to), but it's also fun to have quality time together and to show them your life.

The thing is, you'd like their visits to be scheduled and finite. How do you discourage unannounced visits? Here are some ideas:

- Turn off all the lights and hide under the bed when they arrive. Next time, they'll have to call first!
- Leave the guest room in a constant state of disrepair. (You may already do this anyway—now you can justify your sloppy lifestyle!)
- Have an open, honest, adult conversation with your parents. (Naturally, I'm just kidding. No reason to think that will work now, since it never has before.)

One particular problem with family visits is that moms, in particular, become overly interested in everything you are doing. They begin to shadow you closely.

I'm thinking of creating a product called "Mom Glue," which allows mothers to physically glue themselves to their children when they come to visit. I have no doubt that such a product would be a big seller (as would be the solvent for ungluing).

While you love having your mother around, a few problems, of course, are created when she glues herself to you. For example, it's now very difficult to:

- Bathe
- Sleep
- Drive a car
- Operate heavy machinery
- Interact normally with other human beings

Your dad, meanwhile, is guaranteed to spend any visit fixing things around your house. This is unbelievably helpful of him . . . until you remember that time he "fixed" the toilet and then the bathroom flooded. After your dad leaves, you should have a full home inspection by a licensed professional, just to be safe.

It's important to remember that all of these tactics come from a place of deep love. For years, your parents got to see you every day. Now it's hard to find the time to see you at all, so when there's an opportunity, they will want to be sure they take it. It's better to have parents who care too much than not at all. And you'll tell your mom that . . . just as soon as she unglues herself from you.

The Peace Process

Eventually, as the hostilities over who spends which holiday with which family spiral out of control, a summit, possibly in Geneva, is required. Here are some points you might want to hold firm on during the negotiations.

Holiday Planning Compromises

1. You will only discuss holidays that are happening in the next twelve calendar months. Every time a parent asks a question about a holiday that is not happening in the next twelve calendar months, those parents forfeit a night with you next Christmas.
2. The two of you will not be expected to consume more than one Thanksgiving dinner on the same day. If you are

required to consume a second dinner on the Friday after Thanksgiving, or the Wednesday before, you will not be given a guilt trip for eating lightly.

3. If your parents suddenly decide they want to celebrate a holiday for the first time in a decade, your nonattendance shall not be subject to a guilt trip for at least three (3) years.

In exchange, here are two areas you may concede to your parents:

1. Once the two of you commit to coming home for a holiday, you agree to purchase plane tickets in a timely manner and shall not, under any circumstances, use that lame-ass "expensive plane ticket" excuse that your siblings always use.
2. You will spend equal time with both sets of parents. However, if anyone wants to bake cookies or brownies in an attempt to make you stay longer, please go right ahead (and don't forget the vanilla ice cream).

After the list of compromises has been signed and approved by the League of Nations, the two of you will of course realize that there is a perfect solution that you failed to bring up in negotiations. Sometimes the fairest thing to do over a holiday weekend is visit *neither* family—that way, no one feels as if someone else is getting preferential treatment. You could spend Labor Day lounging around your house, just the two of you. You could spend Presidents' Day getting a massage. You could go to the movies on the Fourth of July. You could just spend New Year's Eve staring at the walls in peaceful silence.

At first you'll feel guilty about feeling this way, but you will soon get over the guilt as you sink deeper into the couch pillows in your blissfully quiet living room.

THE PERFECT SOLUTION

If the two of you happen to be from the same city, there is another solution for holiday times: sharing the time and seeing both families. You can either make room at one Thanksgiving dinner table for both families or you can split the day between them. Isn't sharing what the holiday is all about, along with football, shopping for Christmas presents, and overdoses of tryptophan?

Or, if your families live in different cities, why not have them both over to your place for the holidays? You'll have to be sure to blend both families' holiday traditions, but that can often create new, improved rituals.

Tradition in Wife's Family	Tradition in Husband's Family	New and Improved Tradition!
Everyone gets to open one present Christmas Eve	No one opens any presents until after brunch Christmas morning	Christmas brunch now held at 7:45 on Christmas Eve and all presents opened immediately afterward
Colored lights on the tree	White lights on the tree	Two trees
Midnight mass	Viewing of the movie *Scrooged* starring Bill Murray	*Scrooged* downloaded onto video iPod for viewing during midnight Mass
Wife's dad carves the turkey	Husband's dad carves the turkey	Lasagna
Singing Christmas carols	Getting drunk by the fire	Loud, festive, and slightly slurred rendition of "The Twelve Days of Christmas"
Jesus	Moses	"Let's just spend New Year's Eve together."

After it's all said and done, you realize that the joint holiday was a raging success. Which means you guys are now hosting Christmas dinner for the next six decades . . . a thought that scares the living crap out of you, but it's too late now.

For the Husband

Visiting the families over the holidays isn't always a zero-sum game—a fact that tends to drive a lot of guys crazy. Most husbands assume that you can spend Thanksgiving with one set of parents and Christmas with the other and everything will be peachy.

It's rarely that straightforward.

Maybe your grandmother wants to see you at Christmas because it's also her eightieth birthday. Maybe you don't have time to travel at Thanksgiving because of a conflict with your job. Maybe your parents will decide that they need you to come home in the spring and dress up as the Easter bunny for all the young kids in the neighborhood. ("Um, Mom, the inside of this bunny costume still smells like Uncle Glen . . .")

You and your wife will find a way to work it all out, but you'll need to be patient. The planning isn't going to be as straightforward as your gut instinct says it will be. In fact, most things in your gut are more complex than you think they're going to be, such as that all you can eat Indian buffet you had for lunch.

For the Wife

Ladies, you need to make time for your husband's family, even if they drive you (and your husband) crazy. Just because your hubby doesn't talk to his mom every day on the phone (the way you and your mom do) doesn't mean his parents should always get the short end of the stick. They're his family, which means they're your family. Embrace them. Even if no one in his family can cook or chew with their mouth closed or tell a story that doesn't involve diarrhea, you will still need to spend Thanksgiving with them at some point.

Maybe you can be the one who opens up a new level of dialogue between your husband and his family. And by "new level of dialogue," I mean "can someone ask Uncle Mel to please not tell the story about how he got syphilis in Vietnam while we're at the dinner table?"

7

Should We Hemorrhage Money on Jimmy Choos, Spend the Day at the Racetrack, or Do Both?

Compromising on Your Vices

Nobody's perfect. Some of us gamble more than we should. Some of us drink more than we should. And some of us gamble on drinking games. When you get married, though, these vices no longer affect only you. Your spouse is now part of the equation. It's both of your futures that one of you is gambling away at the craps table. And it's both of your reputations that are tarnished when one of you gets embarrassingly drunk at a party.

One Man, Many Vices

Husbands, you'll quickly find that your vices can be separated into four categories:

Category 1: Activities You Already Knew Were Vices

These vices are fairly self-explanatory, but just in case you need some clarification, I'm talking about the usual guy stuff, such as:

- Smoking
- Drinking
- Gambling
- Racketeering
- Treason to the Crown

Presumably you've already been working for years at curing these vices. I don't mean to sound flippant. Some of them, such as drinking, are really serious. But these vices soon pale in comparison to the second, and far more important, category.

Category 2: Vices That You Didn't Know You Had Until Your Wife Pointed Them Out to You

The underlying problem with these vices, of course, is that you've just recently become aware of them. You have no idea how to cure them since oftentimes you didn't even know they were vices to begin with.

Here are some examples of what I'm talking about.

Example: Reckless Driving

You have always considered yourself to be a safe driver, because in your mind "safe" means "fast." You consider your high auto insurance rates to be a compliment. But not long into your marriage, this conversation occurs:

Wife:	I'm worried about your reckless driving.
Husband:	I'm not a reckless driver!
Wife:	You just drove sixty-five in a twenty-five-mile-per-hour zone.
Husband:	Everyone does that.
Wife:	It was a school zone.
Husband:	It's summer.
Wife:	You hit a child on a bike.
Husband:	I did? Oh, my God! [*pause*] Is the car okay?

Example: Fantasy Football

How is this possibly a vice? Sure, you spent so much time checking stats at work that you got fired and then when you came home you didn't tell your wife, because you needed to go to your computer and check the injury reports. And then when your wife came in to talk to you about your antisocial behavior she tripped and broke her ankle, but you couldn't drive her to the hospital because you had to finish making your substitutions before the 4.00 p.m. East Coast start of the Giants game. But, still, you just don't see what the problem is.

Example: Falling Asleep in the Middle of an Important Conversation

Husband: What? Come on, baby! I never [*snoring sound*].

So how do you begin to cure yourself of these vices you never knew you had? Just ask your wife! She will have *plenty* of suggestions, like:

- "Don't do these things ever again."

and

- "I'm not kidding."

Category 3: Activities That Aren't Vices Yet but Could Be Soon

- Your tendency to invest large sums of money in a snack food company because it makes delicious BBQ-flavored chips.
- Your tendency to ignore infant children in favor of wasting time on Wikipedia.
- Your tendency to fix all home problems with Drano (including those problems that aren't really plumbing related).

One tip for solving these vices is to check with your spouse before you do, well, anything.

Category 4: Miami Vices

These include:

- Driving in a Lamborghini with another guy
- Wearing a white blazer
- Disobeying your lieutenant because you know your instincts are right
- Living on a boat with a pet alligator
- Making love while a song by Phil Collins plays in the background

Luckily, these vices don't require a solution, because they are so damn cool (and they will be back in style again eventually).

I Am Woman, Here Are My Vices

Ladies, you have your vices as well. What? Me?! Yes. You. Female vices fall into two categories:

1. Vices that resemble those that husbands suffer from
2. Shoes

The vices in category 1 are not a problem because of the very fact that your husband suffers from them as well. Truth be told, these vices are probably part of the reason you fell in love. You figured you'd draw strength from each other as you both tried to quit racketeering (it's just so damn addictive, though!).

When it comes to category 2, I'm obviously being stereotypical. Not every woman is obsessed with shoes. But every woman is more obsessed with shoes than her husband is (although that's not too difficult to accomplish, since your husband has exactly two pairs—black shoes that are ten years old and barely broken in and sneakers that are so dirty they classify as a biohazard).

But at some point—now that your finances have merged—your husband is going to figure out that women's shoes are very expensive. When this happens, he'll instantly label shoe shopping as a vice, mostly because he has seventeen vices himself and will feel better if you have a couple to counteract his.

The good news, ladies, is that you can easily confuse your husband because he doesn't know that much about shoes. So when he asks you certain questions about shoes, there are a couple of smart answers you can give.

Question That Your Husband May Ask You about a Pair of Shoes	Answer You Should Give	Reason This Answer Is Technically True
Are those new shoes?	No.	You've been wearing them all day. They're hardly new anymore.
How much did those shoes cost?	$49.99	They did cost $49.99 . . . in 1965.
Can you return them?	Yes.	You could indeed return them . . . if you were a fool.
Don't you have a pair exactly like these?	No.	That other pair he's thinking of are linen white while these new ones are taupe.
Are they at least comfortable to walk in?	Yes.	They look amazing and that makes you feel comfortable (even as blood drips from your heel).
Are you going to wear them more than once?	Yes.	You have every intention of wearing them more than once. Unless you find other new shoes that you like better.
Do you even have room in your closet for another pair of shoes?	Yes.	You've commandeered half your husband's closet.

What you'll soon discover is that your husband's awareness of your shoe vice has an upside: he's actually noticing your shoes! Having such a fashionable spouse makes you proud. And just as you think that, you see him intentionally wipe ketchup on his pants.

A couple of other vices may also spring up as offshoots of the shoe addiction. These include:

- Debt (because you buy shoes you can't afford)
- Antisocial behavior (because you only want to spend time with the shoes)
- Cattiness (toward women who own better shoes than you do)
- Addiction to painkillers (from wearing amazing shoes that don't actually fit)
- Larceny (when you just *have to have* those shoes)

And, of course, the most common offshoot of them all:

- The need to buy Other Stuff

Now that you have nice shoes, it's time to get going on the rest of the outfit:

Clothes

Clothes aren't really a vice because, hello, you'd be naked without them. And if you're going to cover up your beautiful body, it should be with equally beautiful clothes. (Lots of equally beautiful clothes.)

Hair

If a man and woman get the exact same cut in a salon, it costs the guy $70 and the woman $325. But that's not your fault, so it's all good.

Bath Products

If a thirty-dollar bottle of moisturizer makes your skin glow, then a ninety-dollar bottle of moisturizer should make you look like Gisele Bündchen, right?

Handbags

Handbags and shoes are similar vices, at least as far as your husband is concerned. He understands the general need for these items: shoes help protect your feet when walking around and handbags allow you to carry everything you own with you at all times, including all your toiletry products, three types of chewing gum, two pairs of sunglasses, and ninety-three tissues.

However, it's hard for a husband to understand why you need more than two handbags. That's because husbands can never seem to grasp that the thrill for women comes from finding, touching, trying on, thinking about, and then ultimately buying the handbag. The actual *using* of the handbag is a secondary consideration.

Unlike shoes, though, the wife has secret leverage with handbags—by carrying the husband's stuff. Once the wife puts her husband's sunglasses case into her bag, she's in control. Any objection from the husband about a new bag purchase results in him carrying around his own sunglasses case or, even worse, carrying around a manbag of his own.

Road to Recovery

Now that you've each identified your vices, it's time to do something about them. Using gambling as an example, here's a basic timeline for how the process will play itself out:

Day One. Husband announces he's giving up poker.

Day Two. Husband wonders if online poker is still allowed under the Day One edict.

Day Five. Husband is now a member of thirty-six online poker sites.

Day Ten. Wife catches husband playing online poker and tells him that the Day One edict bans such things. Husband says he'll give up online poker that afternoon.

Day Fifteen. Husband gives up online poker after wife catches him again.

Day Twenty. Husband tries to convince wife that playing blackjack is totally different from playing poker.

Day Twenty-one. Husband repeals Day One edict.

Day Twenty-two. Husband enters and wins poker tournament.

Day Twenty-three. Wife takes up poker to pay for new shoes.

As you can see, kicking a vice can be a very difficult proposition. The failure to do so causes several problems: you are still a gambling addict and, even worse, your spouse is now better at poker than you are. As for the spouse, you are faced with a dilemma: should you let your husband win a few poker hands so he feels better about himself? Of course I'm just kidding. If he can't read your bluffs, then to hell with him.

You can also experiment with a solution called "Vice Substitute." Under this strategy, you replace your vice with something else. The trick, of course, is to make that something else much less harmful than the actual vice. There's no point in giving up tobacco and replacing it with, say, opium.

Ideally, the vice substitute will be a beneficial activity as well, not just the lesser of two evils. But addictive behaviors are hard to break.

Vice	You Could Replace It With . . .	But Don't . . .
Gambling	Volunteering at an old folks' home.	Start betting on bridge games.
Drinking	Reading literature.	Read anything by Hunter S. Thompson.
Excessive shopping	Working at Goodwill.	Buy back the clothes you just donated.
Biting your nails	Jogging.	Jog by the manicure place.
Short temper	Yoga.	Blame your instructor for trying to teach you stretches that are goddamn impossible!

All of this leads to one very scary question:

What if you try to kick a vice and fail?

It's frustrating for both people in the marriage. The person who's trying to quit is obviously going to be annoyed at how difficult it is to stop. But, in many ways, the situation is just as hard on the spouse. The spouse is the coach, and when you lose the big game, the coach is just as disappointed as the player.

And yet, fair or not, it's usually up to the coach to stay positive. Your addicted spouse is feeling down about him- or herself, and this is the moment for you to shine.

You can support your spouse in these hard times through a balance of encouragement ("You went a whole week without gambling!") and tough love ("You are terrible at poker. If you're going to lose money, at least find a game you're good at."). Only you will know for certain which method is best for your spouse.

A KEY DISTINCTION

It's very important to realize the difference between a vice and an annoying personality trait. If you're not sure what I mean, here are some examples.

Vice	Really Annoying Personality Trait
Smoking pot	Repeatedly doing Christopher Walken impressions when high
Drinking too much caffeine	Arriving at the front of the Starbucks line without having given any thought to what you want to order
Short temper	A complete inability to eat movie popcorn without getting 73 percent of it on your shirt . . . and then getting pissed at the popcorn
Interrupting people when they're in the middle of a conversation	An insistence on quoting lines from *Caddyshack* once the quoting-*Caddyshack* moment in the conversation has clearly come and gone
Picking your nose	Flinging snot at people and yelling *"Gooooooal!"* every time you hit someone
Eating too many deep-fried foods	Clapping every time a waiter drops something in a restaurant

The reason you need to make the distinction is because vices can be cured. Personality traits are, in theory, the reason you fell in love with your spouse. Hey, don't look at me. I didn't marry someone who doesn't know what she wants at Starbucks.

For the Husband

It's really nice to reward your wife when she makes progress in kicking a vice. Even if she hasn't reached the ultimate goal, positive reinforcement goes a long way toward helping her get there. So, if she's gone a month without smoking, buy her a little present, make her a nice dinner, or take her to the movies. It doesn't have to be fancy—just a little treat to encourage more good work. FYI, there is a 99 percent chance that your wife will want her little treat to be shoes, even if that's the vice she just kicked.

For the Wife

You need to have patience with your husband when he's kicking a vice. Actually you need to have patience with him all the time, which should have been painfully obvious from the moment you met him.

With vices, though, your patience is especially needed. You're not going to make over your man overnight. In fact, if you want to, that's probably a bad sign. Remember: your husband isn't a project; he's your companion.

Think of your husband as a house. You are allowed to give him a fresh coat of paint and change out the furniture now and then. But if you're constantly trying to pour a new foundation or replace the roof, you're in serious trouble.

8

Is "Losing" the Checkbook the Same as "Balancing" It?

Combining Your Finances

Bankers are fairly serious people. They have to be. They deal with large sums of money and the high risk involved with lending it. And so, to lighten the mood, bankers created the joint checking account, which provides more comedy than the slippery banana peel, the pie in the face, and "Take my wife, please!" ever could.

How?

Well, sooner or later, a customer comes barging into the bank and says, "I never wrote this check for $3,500!" The teller looks up the check on his or her computer and says, "Hmmm . . . it seems your spouse wrote that check." The embarrassed customer skulks out of the bank and the tellers get to spend the rest of the day laughing and doing impressions of the angry customer.

Despite the fact that you become bank teller fodder, most couples find a joint checking account to be one of the most helpful financial undertakings of their marriage (the other being the sudden discovery of crude oil under your house). If the two of you are still on the fence about the joint account, consider the following pros and cons.

Joint Checking Account:
Pros vs. Cons

Pro	Con
Monthly bills are now easier to pay because you have one checking account for all those expenses.	Monthly bills are still difficult to pay because each month you must tear the house apart looking for the checkbook after one of you misplaces it.
You can each deposit a chunk of your salary in the joint account while keeping a certain percentage for yourself in your own account.	Debate about how much of your salary you should each contribute to the joint account lasts a minimum of forty years.
If one of you is good at finances then the other will have a balanced checkbook for the first time in his or her life.	If you're both bad at finances, you'll now have an extra account to mismanage.
You can pick a fun background image to appear on your checks.	One of you orders the "Teddy Bear Heart" design without checking with the other.
Either of you can write checks from the account.	Confusion ensues when one of you keeps detailed records of every transaction and the other writes things like, "$500 or maybe $1200????"

In the end, most couples get the joint checking account for peace of mind. If you don't have one, then anytime something goes wrong financially, you'll wonder if the problem could have been avoided with the help of a joint account. In fact, anytime something goes wrong that *isn't* financial, you'll wonder if the joint checking account would have helped ("I can't believe I forgot my mom's birthday! This never would have happened if we had a joint checking account!").

Once you open the joint checking account, the next step usually is to get a joint credit card. Only the decision to cultivate a beehive in the bedroom could lead to greater conflict. The two of you will have long debates about what classifies as a joint expense. When the first joint credit card bill arrives, the following conversation will take place:

Wife:	Sweetie, what's up with this charge from Al's Liquor Store?
Husband:	Oh. I picked up some beer for the house.
Wife:	Hmmmm. I don't drink beer. Is that really a joint expense?
Husband:	It's food and drink, which we said was a joint expense. I mean, I don't eat fruits or vegetables, but I don't complain when you buy them at the grocery store.
Wife:	Okay. You have a point. I think. But what about this charge at Macy's?
Husband:	Underwear.
Wife:	How is that a joint expense?
Husband:	I wear it to excite you.
Wife:	You wear tighty-whities.
Husband:	But you have to admit, as tighty-whities go, these are pretty exciting. Am I right?
Wife:	[*Ignoring last remark from husband*] And what about this charge from the Chicago Bulls? You went to that game with Ted.
Husband:	Originally, when I bought the tickets, I was going to take you.
Wife:	What happened?
Husband:	I asked Ted first and he was free.

Before the insanity gets (further) out of control, here are some ways for the two of you to make your peace with the joint credit card.

Solution 1: Captain's Picks

Each of you agrees to try to be as responsible as possible, but you also agree that you each have two captain's picks each month. What's a captain's pick? It's a charge that isn't technically a joint expense, but you'll both agree to let it slide. As long as it's under fifty dollars. And not illegal.

Solution 2: Agreed-Upon Venues

Limiting the scope of where you can use the joint credit card cuts back on the number of potential conflicts. So you both agree that the joint credit card is for use at grocery stores, restaurants, hotels, airlines, and doctor's offices. This works great, until one of you (I'll let you guess which one) starts buying sports tickets through a hotel concierge in your hometown under the theory that it is a "hotel expense." Wives, should your husband do that, you can then feel free to go to same hotel and treat yourself to a spending spree at the lobby shops.

Solution 3: Go Crazy with It

At this point you're married, so all the money is basically going into the same pot. So one way to stop arguing about what goes on the joint credit card is just to agree to put *everything* on it. Bath salts? Magazines? Burger King? Yes, yes, and yes! Eventually, you'll get annoyed when someone *doesn't* use the joint card. Why did you pay for that hot dog in cash? It's a joint expense!

Whatever solution you pick, you still must confront the normal issues that surround a line of credit:

Credit Card Problems You May Already Suffer From (Which Only Get Worse with a Joint Card)

- Citibank doesn't consider the line "I know I have the bill somewhere in the living room" to be a valid excuse for untimely payments.

- In order to dispute a charge, you need to have the receipt from the transaction, which, um, might be on the floor of your car (if you're lucky).
- Losing a card is hard enough; when you *both* misplace your cards, the headaches are doubled, and American Express is going to think you're both really dumb.
- Every time you buy something that you probably shouldn't, there's a computer somewhere that remembers what you did for the rest of time. And the computer will share its knowledge with your spouse . . .

The real difficulty with joint expenses, though, comes when the two of you make major purchases together. There was the potential for this to have been a problem back when you were decorating your home, but the husband was too confused to understand what was happening. He spent those days thinking things like, "Seven thousand dollars seems like a lot for a coffee table, but, seriously, what the hell do I know? If we just buy it maybe I'll be allowed to go home."

But now the husband has found out the truth about coffee tables. It happened accidentally, of course, when he spilled some beer on the Newburys' coffee table and offered them a check for seven thousand dollars—only to have John Newbury explain that the coffee table cost only twenty-seven dollars at IKEA (although it took John a week to assemble).

As a result, the husband is not getting the wool pulled over his eyes again. Now, when the two of you buy a very expensive item, you'll need to confer with one another. Not surprisingly, your opinions may differ.

Very Expensive Item	Husband Says . . .	Wife Says . . .
Car	Porsche	Prius
China that you didn't get off your wedding registry	Wait. What did we decide about the car?	Prius. And don't ask again.

Giant new TV	This will be great for watching the Super Bowl, and, also, you know, that DVD of *The Joy Luck Club* that you own.	Buying General Motors would be less expensive.
Refrigerator	Frankly, I'd rather have a TV.	Yeah, who needs refrigerated food? Oh, that's right, all modern humans do.
Couch	What's the point of having a new couch if there's no TV to watch when you're sitting on it?	If you say one more word about the TV, we're not having sex for six months.
New bedroom furniture	Whatever you want to do.	Thank you.

The wife has wound up with the items she wanted and the husband has stood up for what he believes in and will also get some sex. Everyone wins!

The Upside

Thus far, I've only discussed some of the hardships that come with combining your finances, but there's also a large upside: combining certain expenses will usually allow you to save money. Your marriage is sort of like an after-Christmas sale: "Come for the true love and stay for the savings!"

Here are some of the great ways that the two of you can take advantage of these once-in-a-lifetime offers.

Car Insurance

Insurance companies usually offer a discount for married couples. If you have separate policies, you can combine them into one. Now when one of you runs a red light, you both pay!

Income Tax

Income tax rates can often be lower for married couples who file together. You'd celebrate this news, except that it's currently April 14 and you totally forgot that taxes are due tomorrow.

Health Insurance

It's usually cheaper for one of you to become a dependent on the other's policy rather than having two separate policies. However, the annoying amount of paperwork required to make this happen means that you'll never do it.

Cell Phone Service

With most providers, it's cheaper to have a single account with two numbers than two separate accounts. And, as a bonus, it lets you argue about who's using up all the minutes.

Membership at the Tennis Club / Yacht Club / Golf Club

If you both have memberships at the same tennis, yacht, or golf club, you are (a) a perfect match for each other and (b) not overly concerned with saving money, which is good, because there are no savings to be had. The only perk is that you can now secretly charge cheeseburgers to each other's accounts—you yuppie pranksters, you!

Of course, the biggest way in which you wind up saving money is simply having someone else that you have to be accountable to. Even if you're not looking over each other's shoulders, there's a certain internal guilt that comes from needless expenses once you're part of a married team. For example, when one of you says, "I bought the toilet paper that was on sale because it meant we'd save thirty-five cents!" the other person is suddenly reluctant to say, "I just spent $412 at J. Crew!"

Much like the president and Congress, you now have a separation of power that provides helpful and necessary checks and balances for financial spending. And when there's a real disagreement, you can always appeal to the third branch of power: your accountant.

You may, at first, be reluctant to hire an accountant or financial adviser, thinking it's a needless cost. But then, as you argue about the cost of the accountant, you realize that you need an accountant to tell you if an accountant is a good expense.

Moreover, if neither of you is feeling particularly savvy about managing your funds (or if you both think you're savvy and thus spend your days having nonhelpful savvy-offs), then an accountant is required.

Accountants fall into the category of things you don't think you need until you have them, at which point they immediately become indispensable.

The cost of hiring an accountant is almost always offset by the numerous ways in which that person saves you money:

Ways in Which an Accountant Can Save You Money

1. Helps avoid IRS penalties by informing you that, unlike Easter, tax day isn't "sometimes in March and sometimes in April."
2. Can improve upon your current investment strategy of "pizza" and "iTunes."
3. Helps you avoid checking account fees by teaching you that Quicken is a better system than recording checks on a napkin (and then throwing the napkin out).

> The process of hiring an accountant is easier than you think it will be. All you have to do is meet with about five people and then hire the most boring one. The more dynamic the personality, the worse the accountant. Every moment an accountant spends interacting with humans is time lost finding ways to save you money. All good accountants should be like NyQuil: if they're not putting you to sleep, they're not working right.

4. Implements radical new plan whereby household bills will be "paid" rather than "used as bookmarks."
5. Knows that $12,301.22 plus $6,843.50 equals $19,144.72 and not just "a lot."

The Bad News

I think you're both old enough to know a secret: frozen broccoli can be just as delicious as the fresh stuff. More relevantly, here's another secret: no matter how many precautions you take, you may still face frustrating financial moments in your marriage. Some of them are your fault and some of them aren't, but they just always seem to pop up, much like acne on a teenager (and you can't just cover up the problem with Clearasil). And, just like zits, they can take many different forms, all of which are kind of gross.

Frustrating Moment: One of You Loses Your Job

The financial ramifications are obvious, but it's important not to kick your spouse when they're down. They're already having a bad day; they don't need to be reminded that losing their job (a) sucks and (b) really sucks. So instead, you try a little optimistic encouragement, with lines like:

- At least we both like SpaghettiOs!
- You were going to quit anyway, you know, when you turned seventy.
- No health insurance means no headaches with the insurance company!
- Did someone say severance package? No? Why not? Shouldn't someone have said that? How could you not get a severance package?

Frustrating Moment: Unforeseen Expense Crops Up

The car accident. The broken bone. The leaking roof. All of these items are annoying, but when you're married, they can wreak havoc on your relationship as well as your checking account.

The best solution for these unforeseen moments is to put aside a small percentage of your income for emergencies. Since you'll immediately forget to do that, here are some other options that you can turn to:

- Return unopened wedding gifts to Crate & Barrel for a store credit, which you can use to get your broken bone fixed at the world-famous Crate & Barrel Medical Center.
- Borrow money from a generous relative. *Warning*: this comes with a required hour-long lecture on financial responsibility, just like that awkward presentation developers make you sit through before they try to sell you a time-share.
- Borrow money from a bank. (It's worth paying the interest to not have to sit through the lecture from your relative.)

Frustrating Moment: Family Member Needs Money

Sometimes the shoe is on the other foot: the two of you have taken good care of your finances, but someone in your family asks to borrow money.

The important thing is that you both check with each other before saying yes. For example, if the husband's brother asks for $2,500 to pay rent, the husband's temptation is to say yes right away. He's your brother and you want to help.

But the husband needs to check with his wife before writing a check. You do this out of respect and loyalty to your spouse, but you also do it to be sure you're not a moron. The wife may point out that the husband's brother still lives at home. So the husband asks his brother why he needs rent money. And the brother confesses that the rent money is really more for "renting a seat" at the Super Bowl. And maybe a trip to Mexico. And pot.

Three Steps to Financial Relief

If financial headaches do come your way, here's an easy three-step program you can use to feel better.

Step 1

Remind yourselves that most of the money problems will go away if you can each quadruple your income next year.

Step 2

Try not to get frustrated when you realize that neither of you is likely to quadruple your income next year.

Step 3

Realize that even if you did quadruple your income, you'd still probably have a disagreement about money anyway, like what make of Ferrari to buy. This makes you feel much better about the fact that you won't quadruple your income. You both walk away happy and with a feeling of accomplishment, even though you haven't really accomplished anything.

For the Husband

Guys, you must allow both your wife and yourself to have a little financial freedom from each other. You can't both be accountable every time you buy a book, a shirt, or a sandwich. You're going to slowly drive each other insane if you e-mail one another with questions like, "Is $2.49 a good price for hummus?"

Consult with each other if you want to buy a house. But trust that you can each responsibly buy shampoo without the other person breathing down your neck.

For the Wife

If you and your husband have a fight about money, make sure that's really what you're squabbling over. Couples tend to have so many disagreements about money that it's easy to use money as an excuse when actually you're upset about something completely different.

For example, if you're frustrated that he bought a thousand-dollar suit without telling you, that's a fight about money. If you're upset that he didn't want your fashion input when picking out the suit, that's a different conversation altogether, usually starting with the line, "Green jackets are for people who have won the Masters, not for people who sell mutual funds. But good choice, champ."

9

Can We Schedule Some Sex for a Week from Wednesday?

The Postwedding Love Life

All single people secretly fear their married sex life. They spend hours worrying about this potential sexual slowdown, even if their premarriage sex life consists of climbing into bed alone and watching a Taye Diggs or Angelina Jolie movie in slow motion on TiVo.

But as all married people can attest, there's simply nothing to worry about. Sure, there may be a slight dip after the honeymoon ends, but that's because most couples front-load the honeymoon with sex. By around day seven of the trip, the decision as to whether you should stay in bed all day or go hit the omelet station at the hotel breakfast buffet becomes a no-brainer because, hello, they have ten different types of cheese.

Many people don't realize that there are positive factors that increase the quality of your sex life after you're married.

Fabulous Wedding Registry Gifts

It's Sunday morning and you have just used your new espresso machine and your new mugs. The wife compliments the husband on picking out a fabulous espresso machine. The husband compliments the wife on her taste in mugs. They stare at each other in admiration . . . and quickly make their way back to the bedroom (where they have new five-hundred-thread-count sheets).

Really Elaborate Wedding

If you had a really elaborate wedding, you likely spent a lot of time planning it. As a result, you have a lot of free time now that the wedding is over. How will you fill that free time? Writing thank-you notes. But there should be some time left over for sex as well.

The Need for Exercise

You'll do anything to avoid going to the gym, won't you?

The Desire Not to Be Those People Who Get Married and Then Never Have Sex

Wife: Sweetie, I want to make love to you tonight. You know, to buck social trends.

Husband: I love it when you talk dirty.

Proximity to Sexual Partner

Let's not forget the most obvious reason of them all: your partner lives with you! Remember when you were single, and every Saturday night you'd have to schlep to a party so you could maybe meet someone? Well, now you've met that someone and they're on your couch! (Although, if it's after 10:00 p.m., they may be asleep.)

Still, this proximity to your sexual partner should not be underplayed. In fact, the more you think about it, the more it makes the concept of not having sex after the wedding seem ridiculous. It must surely be some sort of silly rumor started by single people.

Now, some nervous single men will also argue that it isn't the *quantity* of sex that decreases, it's the *quality*. That is, before the wedding you can have three-ways and orgies and one-night stands and after the wedding you have missionary-position sex with the same person for the rest of time.

It's an attention-grabbing argument, but one that ignores an important reality:

Important Reality about Men's Premarriage Sex Life

Most dudes did not have three-ways and orgies when they were single. Instead they spent a lot of time thinking about how cool it would be to do those things . . . and then they went and played video games.

Most men talk a big game, but at the end of the day, they know who butters their bread and on which side (namely, the side of the bread buttered by their wife, which, frankly, is kind of a weird image).

And besides, familiarity with your sexual partner makes it easier to be frisky. It's the same principle by which, when you buy an annual pass to a ski resort, you wind up going more often. You know where you're going and you know what you're doing. Or, more to the point, you both know where you're ticklish; you both know whether the lights should be on or off; you both know to hold your cell phone calls or risk being kicked out of bed.

There's a reason no one ever waxes poetic about how the first time they slept with someone they wound up accidentally banging their head on a bedside wall sconce, because those moments are terrible. With a spouse, those moments are less frequent . . . or, at the very least, funnier.

Now, to be fair, there are some negative factors that can come into play as well.

Recent Acquisition of Flat-Screen TV and Satellite Dish

At first, there's simply no time for sex, because the husband needs to spend every waking moment during the next three weeks hooking up the home entertainment center. Then, when he's done, wouldn't you know it—football season has started!

Moving to a New Apartment or Buying a House

Sex is difficult because the wife has no idea where she put (a) her sexy lingerie, (b) her bed, and (c) her husband.

Injury Sustained during Previous Evening of Sex

Sounds much better than saying you threw out your back trying to move the coffee table, which is what really happened.

Exhaustion

When you were young, you could run from Seattle to Boston and still be in the mood for sex. Now, the walk from the bathroom to the bedroom drains the life out of you.

Large Amounts of Business Travel

It's tough to make love when one of you isn't there. Hello, Taye Diggs or Angelina Jolie movie on TiVo!

The good news is that some of these negative factors can turn into positive factors. How? Well, your new TV may work great for a while and then, out of nowhere, static appears. The husband tries to fix the problem himself; then he calls the cable guy; then he calls the TV manufacturer. No matter what he does, the lines don't disappear. Eventually he just gives up on the TV and begs his wife for sex to distract him from the stress of the situation. The wife quickly agrees, because she was the one who climbed up on the roof and sabotaged the satellite dish.

At the end of the day, of course, all couples are different. So to help gauge how each of these positive and negative factors will affect your particular relationship, I've created a little test you can take.

Marriage Sexual Activity Test

Answer true or false to each statement.

1. At least one of you is employed in a job where you actually have to do something besides get the high score on Minesweeper. T or F
2. At least one of you is a mammal who requires sleep. T or F

3. At least one of you occasionally thinks about being a productive member of society. T or F
4. You reside somewhere other than a college dorm room. T or F
5. You have children. T or F
6. You have several children. T or F
7. You have several screaming children. T or F
8. You live with your parents. T or F

Okay, now count up the number of times you answered "True" to a question. Here's the answer key:

You Answered "True" to 0–2 Questions

Congrats! Your sex life will improve dramatically after your wedding . . . at least for a day or two, anyway, until you realize you have no job, no source of income, and haven't slept in a week. Have fun!

You Answered "True" to 3–7 Questions

Like the vast majority of married couples, you guys lead hectic lives, but will still find time for romance . . . as long as it's scheduled ahead of time.

You Answered "True" to All 8 Questions

Think of sex like that pot of gold at the end of the rainbow—it may exist, but for now, you just don't have the time to find out.

King of the Bed

Regardless of how you score on the test, an amazing bedroom surprise awaits you like all married couples. That's right: it's time to go out and buy yourselves a king-size bed.

Now, some of you may be skeptical. You may claim that you really enjoy your existing queen, full, or (God help you) twin mattress. Well, guess what—if you've only ever had powdered milk, you may think it's the tastiest beverage in the world. But once you try out the real thing, you're never going back.

Even if your bedroom isn't large enough to accommodate a king-size mattress, I suggest you simply move your dresser and bedside tables into the kitchen. Your bedroom may be 99.3 percent mattress but that's totally fine.

If buying a new bed seems like a giant hassle and expense, well, um, it is. But the nanosecond you climb into your new king bed you will suddenly understand why it was made for married couples. On the nights you two are feeling frisky, you now have a gargantuan amount of square footage on which to get busy. Falling out of bed when you try to roll over is way too sophomore year of college for you to deal with at this point in your life.

But even more significant is what the king bed provides on the nights when you aren't in the mood. For the first time in years, you each have enough space to spread out and get a solid's night sleep. When you awake in the morning, you may have a strange feeling. It's called being well rested.

Some of you may say that sleeping so far apart doesn't sound romantic. Remember: even though the bed is big, you can still have a little cuddle time in the center of the bed. And then, thirty-five seconds later, you can say, "I love you so much . . . that I'll be right over here on my side of the bed if you need me."

SPECIAL GUESTS

Although the bed is a safe haven for the two of you, sometimes the haven has special guests in the form of your pet or child (actually, I guess there could be a wide range of "special guests" in your bed, but I leave that to your discretion).

Obviously, there's no problem having your pets or kids

join you in bed (unless the kid is, say, seventeen). But make sure that you give your spouse as much attention as you give your pet or child. You are both smart, mature people with highly developed brains, and yet, you can still feel neglected. So every now and then put Junior in his crib and Scruffy in the living room and have a little time in bed just the two of you.

Keep the Love Alive

The king bed isn't the only way to keep your love life energized, although it is one of the most expensive and complicated, so why would you need anything different?

But just in case: there are a variety of other things you can do to keep the love alive.

Way to Keep the Love Alive	Pro	Con
Designate a couple of weekends each month as "romance time."	You'll never go more than a few weeks without making love.	Appointment sex. How romantic.
Buy sexy new lingerie for the wife.	Husband will be aroused.	Husband will be unaroused when he learns that sexy bra cost $85.
Get husband's back waxed.	Wife will be aroused by husband's new, clean back.	Just wait until the back hair grows back, even thicker than before.
Buy a kama sutra book.	Exotic new positions . . .	. . . that you'll never be able to get into.

Eat a lot of chocolate.	You'll do crazy things when you're on a sugar high.	Like develop adult-onset diabetes.
Watch a porn movie together.	Secretly, husband thinks his wife will be into this.	Not so secretly, she isn't.

For the Husband

Men, if you are unhappy with an aspect of your love life, you have to feel like you can speak to your wife about it. Talking to your buddies or your Tiger Woods bobble-head doll is not helpful since, ideally, you're not having sex with them.

Obviously, there are good ways to bring up the topic ("I'm so ridiculously attracted to you, honey!") and bad ways ("Do me!"). But saying nothing will cause even more problems in the long run.

Now, merely asking for something doesn't mean your wife will (or should) drop everything and have sex with you.

Husband: Can we videotape ourselves having sex?
Wife: No.
Husband: Why not?
Wife: Well, for starters, we don't own a video camera.
Husband: Interesting point.
Wife: And besides, you saw what happened to Paris Hilton.
Husband: [*too excited*] Several times!
Wife: Look, we can have more nonvideotaped sex if you want.
Husband: Really? That's actually all I wanted.
Wife: Then why did you ask about the videotaping?
Husband: [*guilty*] I just wanted to buy a digital video camera.
Wife: Ah.
Husband: So can I . . .

Wife:	No.

So, bottom line: you never know unless you ask. Except in the case of videotaping, where the answer is always no.

For the Wife

Ladies, it's important not to get in the habit of using sex as some sort of reward for good husband behavior. It's tempting, I know, because your husband will sit down and cure famine if it meant he'd get to see you naked later that night. But once you start using sex as a manipulation tool, it's tough to stop.

Wife:	[*during sex*] Do you love me?
Husband:	Of course, sweetie!
Wife:	How much?
Husband:	A million percent!
Wife:	Last week it was a billion percent.
Husband:	Huh?
Wife:	Are you saying you only love me one one-thousandth as much as you did last week?
Husband:	How are you able to do math so well during sex?
Wife:	Answer me!

As you can see, it's really weird if you only want to have manipulation sex. And, frankly, there's no need to do it. Remember: he married you. I think it's pretty safe to say that he's not just looking for a one-night stand.

10

Wouldn't Sleeping in the Guest Room Help Your Cough Go Away?

What Happens When One of You Gets a Cold

It's the dead of winter. You've caught a terrible cold. And at the moment, as your body shakes from the chills and your sinuses pound like a kettledrum, all you can think is, "I'm glad I'm the one who's sick and not my spouse."

Sweet sentiment, right? You're biting the bullet and taking one for the team. Um . . . not really.

As awful as it is to be sick, it's even more awful to be taking care of the person who's sick, and that's what your spouse is going through right now. Your spouse would love nothing more than to change places with you. But, alas, he feels fine, which means he's relegated to used Kleenex cleanup duty for the next three days. Swell.

I Want My Mommy

By far the most annoying illness situation is when the husband catches a cold and the wife feels fine. If being a wife were a paid job, this is the moment when everyone would agree that she's "earning her money." But since you don't get paid to be a wife (except in romantic comedy movies), this is the moment where everyone instead agrees that she's "totally screwed."

A husband's illness progresses in six stages, each one of which is more ridiculous than the next.

Stage 1: Making Idiotic Denial That He Is Sick

A guy wakes up in the morning and finds that he has a temperature of 103 degrees. He's sweating. He has trouble breathing. There's fluid in his chest. And what does he say? "I'm fine. I'm going to work."

What's particularly hilarious is that 362 days a year, when he's feeling just fine, the husband is searching for reasons not to go to work. But now that he has the most legitimate excuse in the world to stay home, he's not the least bit interested in using it.

So, naturally, it falls to his wife to alert him that he needs to get back into bed or else he may be hospitalized.

Husband: I'm fine. I just need to get a glass of orange juice.
Wife: You're not fine. You have a fever.
Husband: Oh! Suddenly you're a doctor, using words like "fever" and "fine."
Wife: "Fine" isn't a medical term.
Husband: Keep talking, Doctor!
[*Husband passes out.*]
Husband: [*muffled*] I'm fine.

The wife then carries her husband—who weighs twice what she does—back into bed. He keeps trying to get up, but by now he's so weak that a little tap on his shoulder sends him falling back into bed.

And that concludes stage one . . . the easy part.

Stage 2: Launching a Weird, Philosophical Monologue about Why He Is Sick

No guy can ever accept the fact that he is sick without a concrete reason. Of course, there is no reason for getting a cold other than the fact that your body was invaded by a bug and that's life. But that doesn't stop the husband from putting in his two cents.

Weird Reasons Guys Come Up With for Why They're Sick

- "It's all this humidity."
- "It was the shellfish I ate a month and a half ago."
- "Even though it's February, I bet this has something to do with pollen."
- "It was that guy I sat next to on the plane. Or that kid I sat next to at the movies. Or that lady I sat next to during the conference call."
- "I knew we shouldn't have switched from low-fat milk to skim."
- "Do you think this cold is somehow connected to my premature balding?"

The wife calmly explains that it was probably none of these reasons. The husband then decides that there is no reason at all why he should be sick, which leads to a temper tantrum. He takes care of himself. He gets plenty of sleep. So why is he sick? It's isn't fair!

This segues nicely into stage three:

Stage 3: Acting Like a Little Boy Who Needs His Mommy

This is the moment when wives, justifiably, go totally bonkers. There is nothing more frustrating than a husband who wants you to be his mommy (hello, Oedipus). Usually, the wife can just remind the husband that she's not a middle-aged woman contemplating Botox, but since he's sick, she has to take pity on him. Sort of.

When Husband Is Sick He Says . . .	His Mom Used to Comfort Him by Saying . . .	But Now His Wife Says . . .
I think I'm dying!	That's just the fever talking, sweetie.	Be quiet and get some rest.
I feel nauseous.	I'll make you chicken soup. It will settle your stomach.	Be quiet and get some rest.

I'm going to get way behind on my work.	I'll help you catch up when you feel better.	Be quiet and get some rest.
I'm scared.	I'll nurse you back to health, darling.	Be quiet and get some rest.
Will you read me a story?	Yes.	Hell, no.

Stage 4: Coming Up With Justifications for Refusing to Go See a Doctor

Stage four begins when the husband announces that there is nothing the doctor can do because it's a viral infection. The wife explains that pneumonia is actually a bacterial infection and can be cured with antibiotics.

> Husbands, if your wife's advice to be quiet and get some rest seems a bit harsh, keep in mind that getting some rest is the quickest way for you to feel better. And being quiet assures that she won't suffocate you with a pillow. See? I told you it was good advice.

The husband then announces that he refuses to take antibiotics because the drug companies just overcharge you for the medication. The wife explains that, fortunately, they have medical insurance, so the cost of getting the antibiotics is ten dollars.

The husband fires back that he'll never be able to get an appointment with the doctor. The wife says she's already called and he's free later today.

Why is the husband acting like this? It's because of a rule that few wives are aware of:

> Guys are petrified that if they go to a doctor when they're not really sick, the doctor will make fun of them and call them a sissy.

There is, of course, a zero percent chance of this actually happening. And yet, every guy has a secret fear that his doctor will morph into a crusty old grandparent who says, "In my day, we cured pneumonia with a stick and some gasoline!" And so, men don't head to the doctor until there's a 300 percent chance that something is really wrong, and even then, we begin the doctor's visit by saying, "My wife made me come."

Stage 5: Denying That He Is Getting Better

When the cold was setting in, your husband insisted on going to work, even though he had a temperature of 103 degrees. Now, his temperature is 98.7, but he insists on waiting for it to drop to 98.5, just to be safe. Amazingly, though, he feels well enough to go shoot some hoops with his friends, because "it helps me get back into my routine."

Stage 6: Feeling Better and Forgetting That He Was Even Sick

This is also known as the amnesia stage. Once the husband is feeling better, he'll immediately deny that (a) he was sick and (b) his wife helped nurse him back to health. Even worse, he'll mock other people who come down with the cold, calling them "weak." The only person to whom he'll admit the illness is his mother, because he's secretly hoping she'll read him a bedtime story over the phone.

You Did This to Me!

If the husband regresses to a little boy when he's sick, then the wife has the shockingly different reaction when she's ill. At the first sign of a sniffle, the wife will become a dictator. The wife puts up with the husband's general incompetence most of the time. But now that she's under the weather, this is simply no time to be inflating her husband's ego.

If the wife wakes up with a sore throat and a fever, she wakes the husband and gives him the following orders:

1. Go to the store and buy Tylenol, NyQuil, ginger ale, orange juice, tissues, and throat lozenges. If you forget any of these

items, you will be sent back again until you complete this task correctly.

2. Locate the heating pad. It's somewhere in the house. You have four minutes to complete this task.
3. Fill the humidifier with cold water. If you fill it with warm water I will knock the humidifier over and make you mop up the warm water.
4. Bring me a bowl of chicken soup. Do *not* use the fancy soup bowls that we got off our wedding registry because those are only for guests. If you don't know the difference between the fancy soup bowls we got off the registry and the everyday ones I got at Target, then you are a sorry excuse of a human.
5. Turn the heat up in the house to a minimum of eighty-seven degrees. If that's too hot for you, leave.

The husband has about 482 questions related to these marching orders, but, when he is about to ask them, his wife gives him a look that says, "I know you're not stupid enough to ask me questions right now." Petrified, the husband quickly salutes his wife and scurries off to the grocery store to buy zinc tablets and a bottle of Coke, neither of which was on the wife's list.

The wife adopts this hostile tone for several reasons. Efficiency, as I alluded to earlier, is a big factor. The wife knows what she needs to get better. She's not looking for the husband's input; she simply needs a foot soldier to carry out her commands. If the husband can't comprehend these orders or disobeys them, the wife won't hesitate to court-martial him and replace him with someone who's more capable (such as her sister). The husband is dishonorably discharged from the marriage and spends his days being paranoid in a cabin in Montana.

The second reason the wife becomes so dictatorial toward the husband when she's sick is because the wife blames the husband for the illness. The husband, as you'll recall, got frustrated when he was sick because he couldn't decide who to blame. The wife has no such problem. It's her husband's fault. He gave her this cold. This is true even if the husband hasn't been sick.

Wife: You did this to me!
Husband: Honey, I haven't been sick.
Wife: Ah! But you were a carrier. You carried the disease home and gave it to me.
Husband: Um . . . how do you know that?
Wife: I'm your wife!

The "I'm your wife" line is, of course, the trump card. There is no reply husbands can offer that will do any good. So the husband wisely apologizes for making his wife sick and then runs away and hides from her.

Once she starts to feel better, the wife will *not* develop illness amnesia like her husband. Just the opposite. The wife will remember every aspect of her illness forever. Thirty-two years later, she'll be able to tell you, in detail:

- The date she got sick
- How long the cold lasted
- The symptoms
- The cure (if any)
- What she was wearing on the day she first felt ill
- What she was wearing on the day she felt better
- How helpful/not helpful the husband was

This last point is no joke. If the husband messes up during his wife's first cold, no amount of good behavior in the future will ever make her forget that "I asked him for chicken soup and he brought me clam chowder." (Although, to be fair to the wife, that was really stupid of the husband. Clam chowder? Are you kidding me, buddy?)

Two Stuffy Heads Are Worse than One

Every now and then, the timing of the illnesses is such that you're both sick at the same time. As you can imagine, this tends to be an unmitigated disaster. You both want to act like Florence Nightingale . . . and instead you both become that little girl from *The Exorcist*. Not good.

Only a couple of solutions will remedy this situation.

Take Care of Each Other

As already noted, this is a terrible idea, because everything will quickly degenerate into a battle over who has the runniest nose.

Fend for Yourselves

This is a popular option because this way neither of you is a burden to the other one. However, one of you must go sleep on the pull-out couch in the living room. It's going to be the husband, of course, but that only adds to the things he can complain about.

Whichever One of You Is Less Sick Acts Like the Healthy One

The best solution. Just take a poll every hour, and whoever is feeling better acts as the caretaker until the next assessment. It's worth noting, though, that it's hard to stop this process once you're feeling better. On a random Tuesday night, one of you will announce that you have a headache, and suddenly the other one is administering an ibuprofen drip for the next fifty-nine minutes.

Employ a Live-In Nurse to Take Care of You

You're hopefully at least five years away from really needing this.

PREVENTION

Once you both recover from your colds, you'll then take steps to be sure that you don't immediately get sick again. It's hardly what your relationship needs at this point, right?

Some of the steps you take will be sane and some of them will be . . . well, let's just say you really don't want to get sick again this year and you're willing to try anything, no matter how crazy.

Rational Step You Take to Prevent Getting Sick	Crazy Step You Take to Prevent Getting Sick
Drink lots of fluids.	Burn a sandalwood-scented candle to ward off evil germ spirits.
Get lots of rest.	Alternate between sleeping with a humidifier and a dehumidifier in the room. Some nights you even use both.
Take vitamin C supplements.	Take lots of zinc. Or is it echinacea? Or folic acid? Or potassium? Or magnesium?
See a doctor if you start to feel under the weather.	See a doctor every day. Just take some blood, man, and do something helpful with it!
Avoid hanging around people who are sick.	Avoid hanging around people altogether, opting instead for a Howard Hughes–like seclusion at the top of your Las Vegas casino.

No matter what you do, catching a cold really comes down to good luck. And let's just say that lady luck often loves a good laugh (and sniffle).

For the Husband

If your wife successfully convinces you to go to the doctor, you should take the medicine the doctor gives you in the prescribed doses. Most guys tend to assume that if one pill makes you feel better, then three pills will make you feel better even faster. This theory works, um, never. As a result, you're back at the hospital getting your stomach pumped while still suffering from the flu.

If you must, have your wife administer the pill in the proper doses to you. You can even kid her that you've always had a thing for nurses, at which point she'll tell you that she's always had a thing for doctors, which you're not. End of fantasy.

For the Wife

Your husband is going to pleasantly surprise you when you're sick. Yes, he's going to make some mistakes. When he cleans the thermometer it will somehow wind up dirtier than before; when he heats chicken soup, at least half of the can will wind up on the floor; when you ask him to buy Tylenol, he will buy vitamin E.

That said, your husband will embrace his role of male nurse. An imperfect nurse is far preferable to an indifferent one. He'll take good care of you and do it all with a smile on his face. He'll do this because he loves you and he wants you to be well. (And because maybe next time he's sick you'll relent and read him a bedtime story. And get him some warm milk. And also a teddy bear.)

11

How Come the Only Dinner Reservation We Can Get Is at the Chinese Food Place?

Valentine's Day for Married Couples

Some would say that Valentine's Day decreases in importance after you're married (although, for the record, all those people are guys).

Here's the logic behind that argument: you've both expressed your love for each other in every possible way—legally, publicly, diamond ringly—and so exchanging Hallmark cards as a sign of love doesn't seem to hold a candle to the gestures you've already made.

But others would counter and say that Valentine's Day grows in importance after you're married. First and foremost, you have a Valentine, which means that instead of hating everyone who's in love, you get to be one of those people in love (and, in turn, be the object of other people's rage—how creepy!).

But the holiday goes beyond making other people feel terrible (although that's probably reason enough to celebrate it). Once you're married and planning to be together forever, it's easy to get caught up in your daily life and forget to tell your spouse how much you love him or her. Valentine's Day provides that important opportunity. And, just as important, it gives you both an excuse to get drunk on champagne, which you haven't done since your honeymoon (when you did it ten days in a row).

Before and After

The philosophy that Valentine's Day is more important after the wedding usually wins out, because both the husband and the wife realize they want to celebrate it. The wife is looking forward to some fresh flowers and a romantic dinner out. And the husband is looking forward to a legitimate reason to ask for sex.

But even with both husband and wife solidly supporting Valentine's Day, it's worth noting that several key changes to the holiday occur now that you're married.

These changes often catch many married couples off guard, so to help stem the confusion, we'll discuss the most significant changes.

Gifts Need Not Now Be a Surprise

Sure, Valentine's Day gifts *can* still be a surprise, but now that you're married they don't *have* to be. Why? Well, let's just say that back when you were still dating, you tried the surprise strategy, and it failed miserably.

The then-girlfriend got the then-boyfriend some fancy cologne, which he never wore because he doesn't wear cologne. The girlfriend knew this, but foolishly thought she could make the boyfriend more sophisticated. For his part, the boyfriend was a little offended, because the gift kind of suggested that he smelled bad. The boyfriend sulked about this for ten minutes . . . and then farted.

Similarly, the boyfriend got the girlfriend a DVD of *The Philadelphia Story*, because he knew she was a big fan of Katharine Hepburn. In fact, the girlfriend was a big fan of Audrey Hepburn. So the boyfriend wound up watching *The Philadelphia Story* alone at his place. He enjoyed the film very much and was even more confused about why anyone would prefer Audrey Hepburn to the very talented Katharine Hepburn.

So, now that you're married, you get to spare yourself all of the drama of giving gifts. The wife points to a sweater in a catalog, the husband points to a fancy bottle of wine in the liquor store, and everyone gets what they want. And for those who love the element of surprise, don't worry—there's still plenty of excitement when the wife opens up her gift and realizes that her sweater is the wrong size (and color).

Of course you can make the gift a surprise, if that's really important to you. But, inevitably, you don't want to sabotage other big-ticket gifts you have in the works for birthdays and anniversaries. Instead, try a slightly cheaper alternative, but be sure it's isn't completely void of romance.

Big Gift You Want to Get Your Spouse for Your Anniversary	Less Romantic Version of Gift, Which You Want to Avoid Giving Your Spouse on Valentine's Day
A beautiful necklace	A book about beautiful necklaces
A cashmere sweater	A T-shirt
A watch	A timer for the oven
Fancy stationery	A paper cube from the airport gift store
A day at the spa	A new container of Head & Shoulders
A trip to France	Cigarettes

There Is Now No Excuse for the Husband Not Giving Flowers

Material possessions are not important . . . except when they are. And Valentine's Day is one of those moments. The wife doesn't want flowers because she's uncertain whether her husband loves her. She wants flowers because she loves flowers.

Before you were married, though, the woman was smart enough not to get her hopes up. Maybe the man didn't understand how important flowers were; maybe he was offended by the 4,000 percent markup in the cost of roses; maybe he took the woman's comment literally when she said, "You don't have to get me anything."

Well, now those excuses are gone. The wife has made it clear that she loves getting flowers. She had the accountant set up a mutual fund to cover the escalating cost of mid-February roses. And, just so there was no mistake, she told the husband, "Get me flowers."

Amazingly, the husband is still confused as to whether he should get flowers. Several years ago, the wife said, "Don't get me anything," and so he didn't, and he got in trouble. Now she's saying, "Get me flowers." Does he take her words at face value? Last time he did that he got in trouble. But maybe she was lying before and is telling the truth now.

The safe thing to do, of course, would be to get flowers, but that strategy never dawns on the husband. Instead, he turns it into the biggest mystery of the twenty-first century: to flower or not to flower?

Mercifully, disaster is averted when the husband talks to his mother on the phone. She tells him to stop being an idiot and to go out and buy some roses. When the husband talks back, he gets punished and sent to his room, so he can think about what he did wrong.

The Choice of Restaurant Now Matters

What many husbands fail to realize is that the restaurant doesn't have to be expensive. If you go to a restaurant that you can't afford, neither of you will have any fun since all you'll be able to do is drink water and split a side salad. When you arrive home you're so hungry that you promptly eat all the roses.

Being married actually gives you more options with the restaurant because you don't need to impress each other with a fancy dinner if that's not what you want. When you were dating, the husband probably felt the need to go somewhere beyond his means (unless he didn't feel like going anywhere at all, in which case he likely didn't become a husband).

But now it's perfectly fine to go to an inexpensive restaurant as long as it's appropriate. What sort of places classify as appropriate?

Inexpensive Venue	Could Be Romantic If . . .	Bad Idea If . . .
Tavern around the corner from your home	They have those old-time leather booths.	You have to get up from the leather booth when "Ace," one of the tavern regulars, shows up.
Neighborhood café	They know you there (take that, Ace!).	An amateur songwriter is playing the guitar in the café and singing a song she wrote called "I Hate the World."
Local diner	You both love chili.	It's the sort of place where the next table over will be occupied by a ninety-three-year-old woman who wants you to taste her coleslaw because she thinks it's too salty and wants the charge for it (35¢) taken off her bill.
Hole-in-the-wall Italian place	There're only ten tables and you've got one of them.	It's actually a takeout pizzeria and as you sit at the table the owner says, "Are you gonna be here all night? Because I got other customers who want that table."
Burger joint on the beach	You live in Miami, it's eighty degrees outside, you can put your feet in the sand, and they serve beer.	You live in Maine, it's four degrees outside, there's a rocky coast with no sand, and the beer is lobster-flavored.

You Don't Have to Celebrate the Holiday on February 14 Anymore

This is maybe the most important change of them all. When you were dating, there was enormous pressure to go out on Valentine's Day—even if it was a Monday and you were both swamped with work. If you didn't go out on the actual day, then everyone would assume the guy was a bad seed, no matter what his excuse.

Boyfriend: I'm going to be in court on Valentine's Day appealing the case of a wrongly accused man who's on death row!

Girlfriend: [*sobbing*] My friends will be so disappointed!

But now that the relationship is fully secure, there isn't the same pressure to go out on the fourteenth. If the holiday falls midweek, it's perfectly fine to wait until the weekend. Or, if the husband waited too long and can't get a reservation anywhere on the fourteenth, it's perfectly fine for him to say, "We're going out on the thirteenth . . . because I want to give you flowers a day early!" (Nice save, fella.)

Let's Stay In

There's actually one additional change to Valentine's Day that happens after you're married: you don't have to go out to dinner at all. Instead, you can stay in and cook.

Now, you can obviously stay home and cook dinner on Valentine's Day before you're married. It works especially well if one of you is savvy in the kitchen. And by "savvy" I mean "knows that a colander is not a vegetable."

But when you were still dating, staying in on Valentine's Day may well have carried with it an ulterior motive, such as the boyfriend being too ashamed to admit that he didn't have the money to go out or the girlfriend being too ashamed to admit that she hated the boyfriend's taste in restaurants.

But now that you're married, things have changed:

- The husband has left his job at the defunct Internet company and taken another job at a not-yet-defunct Internet company, so everyone knows he can afford to pay for a nice meal out.
- The wife is now so in love with her husband that whichever restaurant he chooses for dinner will be fine by her. Fortunately, the wife is also comfortable enough with the husband to just tell him which restaurant they should go to.
- You have 4.3 billion pieces of brand-new cookware from your wedding registry.

The first two items would suggest that going out to dinner is the smart move, so you ignore these facts and decide to put all that new cookware to use and whip up a Valentine's Day dinner.

Here's how that decision typically goes:

1. Wanting to make something special and worthy of the occasion, you crack the spine on a very fancy French cookbook that someone gave you as a wedding gift.

   Husband: Who gave us this cookbook?
   Wife: The O'Malleys.
   Husband: Who are they?
   Wife: I'm not sure.

2. You find a recipe for lobster soufflé in the French cookbook and rush off to buy two Maine lobsters. For the cost of those two lobsters, you could have had a ten-course tasting menu at the fanciest restaurant in town.
3. When you get home, you suddenly notice that the recipe in your fancy French cookbook calls for slicing the lobster in half *while it is still alive*. You're then supposed to scoop out the brain and innards and poach them in butter and duck fat. *Mon dieu!*

4. Since you (thankfully) don't have any duck fat, you decide to boil the lobsters instead. You tell yourself that this is a more humane way for the lobster to die, but even the lobster knows it's semantics. At least you get to use your new giant pot!

5. The pot isn't big enough for both lobsters, but you cram them in anyway. There's one claw that sticks out of the water, which is the creepiest thing you've ever seen.

6. You have no idea how long you're supposed to cook the lobsters, so you decide that they're done when (a) they turn bright orange and (b) they're hot enough to melt your flesh (a lesson learned the hard way).

7. You've been so busy with the lobsters that you realize you haven't bought anything else to have with them. A search of the freezer reveals frozen french fries, which you decide would go perfectly with the lobster since you are, after all, cooking a French recipe. Or at least you were, until the recipe freaked you out.

8. While the fries cook in the oven, you set the table with your fancy china, silver flatware, and crystal stemware. At this point you realize that your wedding registry isn't complete since you only seem to have one wineglass and no forks.

9. The husband goes to plate the lobsters, but their temperature is still 942 degrees, so he drops the lobster violently onto the plate, causing the plate to crack. Ten minutes of silence follow.

10. Amazingly, the lobster itself didn't crack—only the plate. And when you sit down at the table (the husband now has a plastic plate) you realize that you don't have any lobster crackers.

11. Nothing else in your house can crack the lobsters. You try knives; you try brute force; you try dropping the lobsters to the ground from a great height. Nothing works. The lobsters have their revenge!

12. An hour later, the kitchen and dining room both look like a war zone . . . but you couldn't care less. You're both in front of the TV in the living room with a bottle of champagne and a half-dozen cartons of Chinese food. It's the most romantic Valentine's Day ever. Later on, you'll think about cleaning up the kitchen and dining room, and decide it would just be easier to move.

13. As you both sleep soundly that night, the fries burn in the oven.

For the Husband

Do not, under any circumstances, complain about Valentine's Day traditions. Yes, some people would argue that if you need a special holiday to remind you to love your spouse, then you're not being a very good husband in the first place. After all, being a husband should be about constant love and support, not overpriced flowers.

That argument is all well and good, except that it's totally wrong. Being a good husband is about constant love and support *and* overpriced flowers (and killing bugs in the house). You can certainly give Valentine's Day your own personal spin when called upon to do so ("I bought you a rosebush for the yard! Now, if only either of us knew how to garden!"). But make sure your "spin" isn't "shunning the holiday altogether," because then your "wife" will be "pissed."

For the Wife

You need to remember to get your husband a gift on Valentine's Day. It doesn't need to be complex—frankly, you could grab a beer out of the fridge and wrap it up and he'd be psyched. But it is a holiday for both of you, and while the emphasis is rightly on the lady, the gentleman wants a little present, even if he's too proud to tell you so.

Getting your husband a gift wasn't as important back when you were dating, since there was a certain coyness that came with Valentine's Day. You pretended to act surprised by everything your then-boyfriend did, who, in turn, pretended that he didn't expect sex in return for getting you flowers and dinner, which, of course, he did.

But now the two of you are officially a team, and everyone on the team wants to get a trophy. In fact, you could probably get him an actual trophy (to go with his beer) and he'd be on cloud nine. He's always wanted a trophy room. Now he can start.

12

A Cruise to Alaska? In November?

Vacationing with Your In-Laws

I talked earlier in the book about the complicated process of divvying up the holidays among your families. But of course there are other occasions when you'll visit with your in-laws, including:

- Birthday parties
- Family reunions
- Sunday dinners
- Unannounced visits
- More unannounced visits
- Seriously, darling, you have to talk to your parents about the unannounced visits
- I'm really not kidding about that

But no occasion provides as much prolonged interaction with your in-laws as when you get invited to go on a vacation with them.

Most of the time, your spouse's family has only good intentions for planning the trip and inviting you along. They want to spend some quality time with you guys while also seeing the world. As a bonus, your host country will reap the financial reward of your tourist dollars, and the endless laughter that comes from watching your in-laws try to speak a foreign language. (*"Je voudrais un cup of coffee, por favor!"*)

On some occasions, though, your in-laws have an ulterior motive for the trip.

Reason Your In-Laws Say They Want to Take the Trip	What They Really Mean
Traveling with you guys makes us feel youthful!	Can you get the luggage?
Since you guys have already spent some time in our destination, you can act as the guide.	That semester abroad was a load of crap, and now we're calling you on it.
We always vacation with the same two couples—this is a nice opportunity to mix it up.	Neither the Hendersons nor the Browns were available.
You speak the language!	You will be working round-the-clock as translator, and will be forced to ask the hotel concierge awkward questions like, "Where can I get a good burger in this lame-ass country?"
We found such a good travel deal that we wanted to include as many people as possible.	We needed a group of four to get the discounted group airfare.

The Great Debates

The vacation with your in-laws usually kicks off with several great debates. Don't worry—there'll be lots more once the trip is under way, including:

- Should we go look at the Sistine Chapel or skip it and get ice cream?
- Should we take a boat cruise down the Seine or stay in the hotel all day and talk about what we want to do?
- Should we hit the slopes, or just sit in the lodge and wait for lunch?

- Should we see Westminster Abbey or go to the Niketown across the street?
- Should we go see the Alamo, or just make the "Let's Remember to See the Alamo!" joke 318 times?

Knowing your in-laws' ulterior motives doesn't mean you're off the hook. You still have to go on the trip. But at least you now know why you were invited. And, as I've stressed repeatedly, knowing what's in store saves you headaches down the road. (But I'd still pack some aspirin.)

Anyway, I'm getting ahead of myself because these issues, as I said, don't come up until you are already standing outside the Alamo.

Before you even go on the trip, certain issues need to be resolved.

Issue 1: Where Are We Going?

In truth, this isn't as complicated as it sounds, because usually your in-laws just tell you where you're going. They'll ask your opinion, of course, in the same way that the U.N. Security Council asks for Iceland's thoughts.

In-Laws: Do you guys have any ideas for the big trip? We're thinking about someplace in Europe!

You Guys: Europe would be amazing. How about somewhere in Italy? Tough to go wrong with that country, huh?

In-Laws: We were leaning more toward Norway.

You Guys: [*long pause*] That could be interesting. Fjords. Vikings. Snow.

In-Laws: We're also thinking about Japan.

You Guys: That's not really in Europe.

In-Laws: Yeah, but we've always wanted to see those temples in Angkor Wat.

You Guys: Um . . . that's in Cambodia, not Japan.

In-Laws: [*long pause*] How about Norway?

Eventually you just defer to whatever your in-laws want to do. Usually this is because they're paying for more of the trip than you are, so they can do whatever they damn well please.

But you also like the idea of deferring to your elders. It's a sign of respect, and the two of you can maybe go to Italy some other time.

So you tell your in-laws that you'll go wherever they want, and they announce that you'll be taking a cruise to Alaska, because no one has expressed any interest in that whatsoever.

Issue 2: Who's Coming with Us?

Your in-laws have extended an invitation to you guys, but then, once the word gets out, everyone wants in on the party.

Who Wants In	Why
Wife's sister	Competitiveness from when they were teenagers has in no way worn off.
Husband's grandfather	Cruise ship = shuffleboard.
Wife's aunt	Hasn't left her house in thirty years and therapist just told her that's kind of weird.
Husband's brother	Has already been on cruise to Alaska and wants to come along so he can sound smart and worldly (even though no one will listen to his random facts about salmon spawning).
Former secretary of state Colin Powell	Retirement is more boring than he anticipated.

The problem, naturally, is that you'd like some of these people to attend, but not all of them. Having Colin Powell could be very handy if an international situation develops with Canada (or polar bears). But then you wouldn't want to include the husband's brother, because he'll spend the whole time telling Mr. Powell about the history of Alaska's bid for statehood (which the husband's brother learned about on his previous cruise to Alaska).

The nice thing is that this issue really isn't your problem. You are mere invitees on this trip and can deflect all hints for an invitation to your in-laws, with comments like, "Oh, we'd love to include you, crazy Uncle Zeb, but that's not really our call."

Eventually, your in-laws pull the deception card out of the deck. They tell everyone else that the ship is full, so there's only room for the four of you. Of course, 271 rooms on the ship are actually empty, because no one wants to go to Alaska at the beginning of winter except your in-laws.

It's a devious way to fix the problem, and it instantly makes you wonder if your in-laws have ever lied to *you*. For example, when they came to stay at your house last year, they said they would have booked a hotel, but there were no available rooms. You always thought that was kind of odd, since you live across the street from a Hilton whose parking lot is always empty.

Issue 3: When Are We Going?

Ask yourself two questions:

- When are the least expensive times of the year to go to the destination we've chosen?
- When is the busiest time at work for myself and my spouse?

Whatever week fits into both of these categories will be the week you're going. Hello, Alaska in the first week of November!

Issue 4: Why Are We Going?

There's really no answer to this question.

Issue 5: How Are We Going?

This one's easier to answer: cheaply and awkwardly.

And Away We Go!

The cruise is departing from Vancouver, Canada, so everyone flies there to meet up for the big adventure. You assume that the only people you'll be rendezvousing with are your spouse's parents, but the final group is larger, despite all the cloak-and-dagger behavior by your in-laws.

Your spouse's grandmother, Eunice, has decided to tag along, because cruises are great vacations for the elderly. Also, Eunice is really upset with your spouse's mother because they both made potato salad for the Fourth of July BBQ and there was way too much. Eunice is on the cruise to relive that potato salad incident a minimum of eighteen times.

Your spouse's cousin Skip and his girlfriend, whose name no one knows, are also coming along, because they live in Seattle, which is near Vancouver, so it seemed weird not to invite them. No one mentions the fact that Skip fell off the radar decades ago, and this is the first anyone has seen of him since the Carter administration.

Cruises, of course, run on very detailed itineraries, so here's how your week plays itself out.

Day 1: In Vancouver

Everyone spends the day walking around Vancouver and admiring the city. In fact, it's so nice that no one's really sure why you'll be getting on a boat and leaving this gem.

Other highlights of the first day in Vancouver include:

- A lengthy debate as to which of the forty-two Starbucks within walking distance of the hotel you should visit.
- A running commentary from your spouse's dad about the rainy weather, just in case no one noticed.
- An announcement from you and your spouse that you'd like to do a little exploring on your own, but that idea is quickly vetoed by the group, who remind you that this isn't about what *you* want to do.

- An hour-long search for Grandma Eunice, when the rest of you realize that no one has seen her since lunch.

Day 2: Boarding the Ship

Even though the boarding time for the ship is twelve noon, Grandma Eunice insists on getting to the docks at 9.00 a.m., so that you can be first on board. You all make fun of Grandma Eunice, but when you arrive at the docks you notice that everyone else traveling with someone over eighty is already ahead of you in line.

When you finally board the boat, you discover that your in-laws and Grandma Eunice have suites, while the two of you are on a different level, which happens to be more convenient to the engine room. However, you're not upset because your room location will afford you a little privacy at night . . . that is, until you realize that cousin Skip and his mystery girlfriend are in the room next to you, and there are adjoining doors.

You and your spouse both agree it's a little silly that you haven't yet figured out this woman's name, so you try to instigate a conversation:

You Guys:	We haven't been formally introduced. We're Ted and Martha.
Mystery Girlfriend:	Nice to meet you.
You Guys:	What was your name again?
Skip:	[*interrupting*] Sweetie, they have that blue stuff in the toilet!
Mystery Girlfriend:	Let me see!

[*Mystery girlfriend runs off; the two of you immediately decide to call her "Blue Stuff" for the rest of the trip.*]

Mercifully, you're saved by the dinner bell. Well, it's not so much a bell as it is the humming of the giant diesel engines one floor below you. But it's dinnertime, anyway.

The ship has multiple seatings for dinner, but because you're traveling with Grandma Eunice, you'll be chowing down at 5:30 every night. You'll also be at the same table, have the same waiter, and, as best as you can tell, eat the same food every night. And even though you're taking a cruise through the Pacific, your entrée options are farm-raised Atlantic salmon or a cheeseburger.

Day 3: At Sea

By about 10:45 a.m., you've exhausted all the activities there are to do on the ship, such as (a) breakfast and (b) looking at the ocean. The brochure advertised a wealth of other activities, but lounging at the outdoor pool doesn't seem all that inviting in the cold rain.

You return back to your room to have a cup of coffee and read the book you brought with you, but Skip and Blue Stuff have decided to have midmorning sex, so you're forced to go see a screening of *Titanic* in the movie theater.

The good news is that the movie is so long, it takes up most of the day. And afterward, you spend an additional hour finding the nearest lifeboat and going over the evacuation plans.

By 5:30 p.m. you're thrilled to be having dinner so early because you're bored to tears. And since it's been dark for three hours, you're actually kind of hungry.

Day 4: Juneau, Alaska

Juneau is sort of like a smaller, colder version of Vancouver, but it's something to do, so you eagerly join Grandma Eunice at the front of the disembarkation line three hours before you pull into port.

The cruise has arranged a nice tour of the city, although the two of you spend most of the day staring at the locals and wondering which of them is in the witness protection program.

After lunch in a local restaurant (which has raised its prices 675 percent with the arrival of a cruise ship), Grandma Eunice heads back to the boat for a nap, and Skip and Blue Stuff offer to accompany her, which is clearly a ruse to go back to their room and have more daytime sex.

The good news is that you guys and your in-laws finally get some quality time just the four of you, which was, after all, the whole point of this trip.

So you walk around in the rain for an hour, with your father-in-law once again providing a running commentary about the weather. Then you look around for a Starbucks, realize there isn't one, and head back to the ship.

Day 5: Adventure Day!

During this day, the ship docks in the middle of nowhere, but the operators call it "the wilderness" to increase excitement.

Your choices for "adventure" include:

- Taking a sea plane to visit a glacier
- Taking a sea plane to visit an Eskimo village
- Taking a sea plane to visit a salmon-canning factory
- Staying on the ship and doing nothing

Everyone wants to do something different, and, amazingly, your in-laws agree that today (and today only) everyone can do what they want.

So you go to see the glacier, your parents see the Eskimos, Skip and Blue Stuff see the salmon, and Grandma Eunice stays on the boat. (However, she still insists on being first in line to disembark, because she hates not being first in line. And when it's her time to get off the ship, she simply steps out of line, heads back to her room, and taunts the other people who were behind her in line.)

The rest of you get off the ship, and quickly realize that you will not actually be spending the day apart, because the glacier, Eskimos, and salmon factory are all in the same village, about twenty feet apart from one another.

The glacier is beautiful, the Eskimos are friendly, and the salmon factory is the grossest thing you've ever seen. Not surprisingly, Skip and Blue Stuff are really into it.

Day 6: Fjords

This day is at sea, but it's a day for sightseeing, not travel. In particular, you have a beautiful view of many Alaskan fjords and, in the evening, the aurora borealis. This is easily the best day of the cruise, for many reasons:

- Gorgeous, breathtaking scenery
- You have a spectacular vista point right on the stern rail because Grandma Eunice shoved other people out of the way
- Your in-laws no longer want to go to Norway, because they're seeing fjords here
- Tomorrow you go home!

Day 7: Extra Day at Sea

There have been some unusually strong winds and currents, probably because arctic winter arrives in twenty minutes. Thus, you need to spend an extra half day at sea just to get back to Vancouver. But don't worry, there's lots to do on the boat, like:

- Being seasick

and

- Pining for the trip to end

Day 8: Back to Vancouver

The last day of the cruise is spent reminiscing about what everyone liked best:

- You guys: the fjords
- Your in-laws: the glaciers
- Grandma Eunice: the fact that meals were included in the price of the cruise
- Skip and Blue Stuff: the fact that they can steal towels out of their bedroom

The Aftermath

Several important things happen after the cruise. First, Skip insists on exchanging phone numbers, which you do, and then you have no contact with him for another eight years.

Grandma Eunice returns to Florida, where she happily gets to describe all the details of the cruise to every person she knows. When she gets through everyone, she simply starts over again with the first friend.

And you realize that it was, at the end of the day, a wonderful vacation. You saw a beautiful part of the world and, more important, you spent some quality time with your spouse's family. You realize that you really lucked out with your in-laws. How nice is it to have relatives that love you and want to vacation with you? Fortune has smiled on you, indeed.

And then, three days later, your own parents call and ask if you want to go on a cruise to Alaska with them next spring. You can already taste the canned salmon.

For the Husband

Whenever you're traveling with your spouse's grandmother, take good care of her. Make sure she has what she needs, and that someone's there to escort her from point A to point B if she needs the help. Remember: she's your grandma now, too, and grandsons look out for grandmas. End of story.

Oh, and by the way, you are *never* allowed to tell her that you've already heard a story. She may not remember that she's told you this story before, but she'll never forget it if you cut her off.

For the Wife

Oftentimes, you'll be able to do everything you want when you're vacationing with your husband's family. But sometimes—especially in foreign countries—you'll be on a tight sightseeing schedule. So if there isn't time to visit a museum you wanted to see or shop in the fashionable part of town, don't worry. You can always return to this destination in the future, just the two of you.

Think of it this way: you will have already done the big sights, and now you can check out some different ones, like a restaurant, a gorgeous cathedral, or that vendor in the town square who makes amazing handbags that cost only ten dollars. Why your in-laws wanted to see Michelangelo's *David* instead of shopping for handbags makes no sense to you at all. Crazy people!

13

Are You Free to Have Drinks with This Friend of Mine Who I Don't Particularly Like (and His Really Annoying Wife)?

The Surprisingly Difficult Task of Merging Your Social Schedules

Before the wedding, the two of you put a freeze on meeting new people. This didn't happen because you were suddenly feeling antisocial. Rather, you wanted to avoid having new friends because then you'd open yourselves up to the possibility of having to invite them to the wedding. You were trying desperately to thin the guest list, not add to it!

So you picked a date—November first, let's say—after which point anyone you met would not be invited to your wedding, which was in March. Inevitably, you were introduced to lots of new people between November and March, and they seemed like the coolest, most interesting people you had ever met. But rules are rules—no wedding invite for them.

After the honeymoon, you will want to attempt to reconcile with these friends, which often plays out as follows:

1. You invite the scorned couple over for dinner, as a peace offering.

2. At the dinner, you both attempt to make no reference to the wedding, which is impossible. So, instead, you try to make it sound as if it wasn't the most awesome party ever (which, of course, it was).

3. After dinner ends, you pretty much never see these friends again, except for awkward encounters at the dry cleaner's or Starbucks.

And so begins your married social life . . .

Singles' Night

Once you're married, there's generally only one group of people you'll socialize with: other married couples. This may not happen right away, but six months after the wedding, look around at your friends. They'll all have something in common, like an incomplete gift registry at Crate & Barrel (when is someone going to buy us some forks?!).

The reason you tend to hang out with married couples isn't because you don't like your single friends. Rather, they have stopped liking you. Why? Because your single friends want to stay up late and do fun things. The two of you, on the other hand, suddenly have different priorities.

When You Were Single You'd . . .	Now That You're Married You'd Rather . . .
Close down bars with your friends.	Be home in bed by eleven.
Sing karaoke until your vocal cords exploded.	Be home in bed by eleven.
Go to a movie that started after 7:40 p.m.	Be home in bed by eleven.
Plan your night around activities besides *Law & Order* reruns.	Be home in bed by eleven.
Stay up as late as necessary in order to have sex that night.	Be home in bed by eleven.

Of course I'm just joking. Sometimes you'll actually stay out until 11:20 p.m. . . . if it's planned well in advance. But even with these restrictions, there are still lots of activities you can do with your single friends.

Eat at the Hippest Restaurant in Town

There's no way you guys would have found this place without your cool single friend. And your cool single friend is psyched because the only available reservation was at 6:30 p.m., and none of her other single friends want to eat that early. You guys, however, are thrilled to have dinner then because when the restaurant turns into a swinging singles scene later in the night, you want to be home taking a bath.

Go to a Concert

You're both excited because you haven't seen Springsteen perform live in a decade. And your single friend is excited because he has a designated driver.

The Group Outing

Several married couples are getting together for brunch. You invite your single friend to join you because it's a win-win situation. The married couples are excited to talk about something else besides being married; the single friend is excited because he's the only guy there who doesn't have to check with someone else before ordering the meat lover's omelet.

Reality TV Night

Invite your single friend over to your place for some trashy TV and takeout food. Afterward, your friend can go out and party and you guys can climb into bed and read a magazine. Everyone wins!

The one thing you should *not* do with your single friends is try to set them up on a date. For some reason, everyone forgets how annoying this is once they get married. Remember: if they wanted to get an earful about being single, they could call their parents.

Couples Therapy

These rare evenings with your single friends aside, other married couples will form the backbone of your social life. The good news is that hanging out with other married couples is extremely fun.

Here's why: each of the married couples you socialize with will fill an important and unique role in your life.

The Couple You're Basically Dating

This is the couple that you see all the time. They're the primary option for Saturday night dinner and trips to Target. Of course, there was that one awkward moment four months ago when you caught them at the mall with another married couple, but you've all agreed to pretend that never happened.

The Couple You Vacation With

These aren't necessarily your closest friends, but they're the perfect traveling companions—they're organized, they like the same category of hotel that you do, and they are incredibly savvy at getting airline upgrades. After the vacation is over, it's completely possible that you will have no contact with this couple until it's time to plan the next trip.

The Exotic Couple

They travel the globe. They cook unusual food. They have a lot of vintage maps on their walls. You feel incredibly worldly after you see them. And after you caught the couple you're dating at the mall with someone else, you immediately made plans with the exotic couple to make them jealous. (It worked.)

The Couple You Keep Thinking You're Going to Be Better Friends with but It Never Really Happens

You keep thinking this couple is going to be promoted into your inner circle of friends, but every time you go out with them, there's always one tiny detail that prevents that from happening—they're moving to the other side of town, they just had a baby, or (most commonly) they just don't really want to be friends with you and are confused about why you keep trying to make plans with them.

The Couple That Doesn't Want to Spend Any Money / The Couple That Wants to Spend Too Much Money

The two extremes of your social life. One pair wants to have you over for rice-and-beans night; the other always orders the most expensive bottle of wine on the planet because they heard this was the best year to drink it. Inevitably they don't really like the wine, but they assume you'll be happy to split the cost with them.

The Couple That's Just a Little Bit More Successful and Physically Attractive than You Guys

Haven't made plans with them in months.

Fred Couples

Maybe he can get you in to play a round at Augusta National.

But by far the most difficult social situation involves the following couple.

The Couple That One of You Likes and the Other One Can't Stand

The more this couple starts to irritate one of you, the more the other will unknowingly want to spend time with them. Eventually, when you come clean about your negative feelings toward this couple, your spouse reacts first with shock ("I had no idea you couldn't stand the Pattersons!"), then with confusion ("Why did you let me invite them to your birthday

> It's worth noting that couples can change categories over time. For example, maybe you've always enjoyed vacationing with the Callahans . . . until Jim Callahan suddenly becomes Expensive Wine Guy on your trip to Australia.

party?"), and finally with anger ("They really are fabulous people. What's your problem?").

In truth, casting your friends as different couples is merely one of many ways that you wind up categorizing your friends. It may seem odd that you spend so much time trying to label your friends, but it's so much more fun to pontificate about your friends than it is to, say, change lightbulbs. So the two of you happily chat about your friends all the time, even as your home slips into complete darkness.

Here are some additional ways that you can and will categorize your friends.

By Days of the Week

"Saturday friends" are your closest buddies and thus you often save the prime socializing night for them. "Sunday friends" are the people with whom you have brunch and walk your dogs. "Wednesday friends" are the people you want to be better friends with, but you're not yet ready to commit to a Friday. And "Monday friends" are the people you like but don't ever see because no one feels like going out on a Monday.

By Geographical Location

The "awesome friends who live on the other side of town" are fabulous people, but it's hard to see them during the week, because, as their name suggests, they live far away. So they've been supplemented by the "friends we're becoming very close to because they live two minutes away." Also worth noting are the "friends who live in another city but we wished they lived here" and the "friends who live in another city but we're actually kinda cool with that."

By Their Jobs

If you feel like going out for a fancy dinner, the "lawyer friends" are always a good bet, assuming they can get off work. The "friends with really cool jobs" are a must at any social gathering, because you seem awesome just for knowing these people with really cool jobs.

And when you want to see a movie last minute on a Tuesday night, you know your "musician friends" are probably free.

By Nickname

Usually these nicknames aren't clever as much as they're just sort of obvious. For example, no New Year's Eve party is complete without Crazy Ted and Chatty Nancy. It's always nice to spend a Saturday afternoon with Mellow Bob and Super Sweet Sarah. And if you're feeling like a gin and tonic, it's best to give Handsome Dan and Preppy Lisa a call.

By How You Know Them

With this method, there's a tendency to sort your friends into three different categories: the husband's friends, the wife's friends, and mutual friends. It isn't always a conscious act, but in the back of your minds, you each have a table that looks something like this.

Person	Category	Notes
Hannah and Gus Anderson	Wife's friend	Hannah is wife's good friend from college. She's also incredibly hot, which means no warm-weather activities with them or else husband will spend the whole day checking out Hannah's ass. Awkward.
Nick McCloud and his girlfriend, Maya	Mutual	Nick works with the husband and he's pretty much the only person from the husband's office that wife can tolerate. Maya is super awesome, which means Nick will probably dump her for someone more terrible.

Steve Crenshaw and his partner, Glen	Wife's friend	Steve is wife's gay friend. He is allowed to touch the wife's breasts more often than her husband can.
Rich Bloomfield and his wife, Mary	Mutual	You met Rich and Mary at a wedding and quickly became better friends with them than you are with the people whose wedding you were both attending.
Lizzy Miller and her husband, Dave	Husband's friend	Lizzy briefly dated husband in college; being friends with her and her husband would be awkward except that the wife loves gossiping with Lizzy about all of the husband's annoying habits. (Lizzy: Does he still snore like a chainsaw? Wife: You have no idea . . .)

The reason all couples subconsciously sort their friends into these categories is because they want to be sure they're splitting their time evenly between the wife's friends and the husband's friends.

Of course, this rationale flies in the face of what marriage is all about. There are no longer "your friends" or "my friends," only "our friends." With that in mind, you agree to stop putting friends into categories. Twelve to fifteen years later, you make good on that pledge.

Truth be told, there's also a fourth category of friends: people that neither of you is friends with. This is different from people you don't know. Rather, these are people you've met a couple of times at various parties. They've very nice and pleasant, it's just that you're not really friends with them. Also, you have no idea what their names are.

But somehow they seem to remember everything about you. As a result, you always feel guilty talking to this couple and pledge that next time you see them at a party you're totally going to remember their names. You don't, of course, so you awkwardly try to avoid them all night, which doesn't work either. Instead, you have a friendly conversation with them as you wrack your brain for what their names could be. Gary and Jenny? Mark and Allison? Andy and Stephanie? Who knows?! So eventually you give them a nickname like Scooby and Shaggy, because she seems to love food and he never shaves.

FRIEND REFERRAL

One of the fun developments that happens in your married social life is when your various couple friends get to know each other and become friends themselves. You're happy that they have new people to socialize with. And, as a bonus, you guys look pretty awesome for having such good taste in people.

That's how it usually goes down, anyway.

Occasionally, though, a friend referral can go bad. It's sort of like recommending a doctor. Most of the time, your friends are grateful for the referral. But every now and then someone returns from your dermatologist with a bad face peel and you never see that friend (or that dermatologist) again.

If one of your more stable couples makes plans with one of your more disastrous acquaintances, things can go bad quickly. To be fair, the Armstrongs were on good behavior the night of your birthday party, so there was no reason for the Jamiesons to suspect that the Armstrongs are secretly bonkers. You would have warned the Jamiesons about this fact, but you only found out afterward that the Armstrongs and the Jamiesons had made dinner plans together.

Now it is too late. Ned Armstrong went on one of his rants

about how the government is watching him and Liz Armstrong got in a huge fight with the waiter about whether there was cilantro in the entrée. Not only will the Jamiesons never speak to the Armstrongs again, but you're also pretty sure they'll never speak to you again.

Friend referrals can also go wrong when two sets of friends start socializing and immediately realize they no longer need the two of you as middlemen.

Secretly, you knew this was going to happen. Remember back in college how you had that one friend you never trusted to be alone with your boyfriend/girlfriend because you were pretty sure they would try to steal that person from you? Same logic applies here. You knew the Winslows and the Cullings would be perfect couple friends. So you selfishly kept them separated as long as you could. But they finally met at your birthday party and now, six months later, they've bought a time-share in Florida together and you haven't seen them since.

Safety Check

Now that you know who you'll be making plans with, you can turn your attention to how you'll be making those plans. This doesn't sound particularly difficult or complicated because you've made social plans for years. All you do is call up your friends, play ninety-six rounds of phone tag, and then go to a movie that no one really wants to see.

Ah . . . but that's how things worked before. Now that you're married, there's one key step you've forgotten.

You need to see if your spouse is free.

It sounds so obvious, right? Well, so do wheels on suitcases, but mankind was around for thirty thousand years before someone thought of those little suckers.

You haven't forgotten that you have a spouse (hopefully). Rather, you just assumed that your spouse was free on Thursday night because he or she has been free every Thursday night for the last seven months. But, inevitably, your mate picked this coming Thursday to catch up with an old friend or get a massage or get a massage from an old friend (hmmm . . .).

So now you have two sets of plans on Thursday. What do you do?

Option 1: You Socialize Separately That Night

No big deal, right? I mean, you and your spouse don't have to spend every night together. The problem is that the people you are seeing secretly like your spouse more than you. They are immediately disinterested in the entire night once they find out that Jane isn't coming, and they pepper the evening with passive-aggressive comments like, "I guess Jane is a very busy woman" and "This night blows without Jane."

Option 2: Combine Your Plans

This is the most convenient option for you, and the least convenient option for your two sets of friends. One of you has made drink plans with the Stollers and one of you has made drink plans with the Cooleys. So you have drinks with everyone, under the premise that you "really wanted the Stollers to meet the Cooleys." However, the Stollers and the Cooleys have already met and dislike each other immensely. Have fun!

Option 3: Cancel One Set of Plans

Great idea. I mean, there's no way this could possibly lead to a disagreement between the two of you.

Option 4: Cancel Both Sets of Plans, Stay Home, and Watch **Goodfellas** ***on HBO6.***

Bingo.

The best way to avoid these scheduling conflicts is to send your spouse an e-mail when making plans to confirm that he or she is free.

Here are some handy templates you can use:

Template 1: Wife E-Mailing Husband

Sweetie:

Are you free on [date of the Super Bowl] to go do [emasculating activity] with my very close friend, [name of friend you haven't seen in twelve years]?

It's a weekend, which means you probably need some time to [household chore husband never does] and then reward yourself by [ineffective attempt to make beer drinking sound sophisticated].

But, still, I'd love to go if we can because last weekend we did stuff you enjoy, like eating [list of disgusting pizza toppings] and watching [name of current HBO documentary about a nudist colony and/or brothel].

Thanks! :)

Template 2: Husband E-Mailing Wife

Hey [nickname your wife has repeatedly asked you not to use]:

Good news! [Name of guy at office who is a terrible influence] just offered us two tickets to go see [activity involving truck with oversize wheels]. He's bringing his wife, and she's finally gotten her [unnerving thing about his wife] under control, so I think we will have a much better time than when we [recap of horrific evening spent with this couple last year].

I know we had said we'd try to go to [name of hospital] that night so you could have [vital medical procedure wife needs to have done] but I just read in [name of magazine on bathroom floor] that [celebrity] had that procedure and now they're [fact about celebrity that in no way suggests postponing the procedure is a good idea].

XOXO

[very cool nickname your wife refuses to call you even though you ask her all the time]

If you don't feel like e-mail is really your cup of tea (because you spilled tea on your computer and now it doesn't work), you can always try to use Post-it notes. Once you make plans, just leave your spouse a little note on his or her desk / pillow / bag of potato chips. But if you go the Post-it route, keep the following things in mind:

1. Neither of you has ever thrown out a Post-it note, so if you just write "drinks on Thursday with the Coopers," it will be unclear to your spouse whether you're referring to this coming Thursday, or Thursday, January 27, 1983.

2. If the Post-it note falls on the floor, your spouse will *not* think, "I bet that Post-it just fell on the floor. I wonder what it says." Instead, your spouse will think, "There's a piece of trash on the floor. Should I throw it out? Nah . . . I'll let my spouse get it." So be sure you stick the note on firmly.

3. If your message doesn't fit on one Post-it, then your plan is too complicated and your spouse's automatic reaction is, "No."

4. If you spell a word wrong, you will be mocked forever. (Unless your spouse also doesn't know how to spell "rendezvous.")

If all else fails, you should just rely on good old-fashioned conversation, which might go something like this:

Wife:	Do you want to have dinner with the Conrads next Friday night?
Husband:	Who?
Wife:	The Conrads. You've met them several times.
Husband:	Really?
Wife:	He's very tall with red hair and he always wears those crazy glasses with the bright green frames. And she's Cambodian.
Husband:	Still can't picture them.
Wife:	We ran into them two days ago at the mall and talked with them for an hour and a half about making plans soon.
Husband:	Still not ringing a bell.
Wife:	She gave me her kidney when I needed the operation. She was in the hospital at my bedside for three months.
Husband:	Are you sure I've met them?

The Hardest Step of All: Leaving the House

Now that you've made (conflicting) plans, there's one more hurdle for you to overcome: actually leaving the house to attend to those plans.

Most people take for granted that walking out of the house will be easy. After all, you've left your house many times over the years, unless you're a crazy person living in the wilderness and hiding from the aliens.

Anyway, back to relatively normal people like you guys. You may have left your house before but, like many things, it gets more complicated with a spouse.

Let's take a hypothetical situation: you're meeting your friends Kristen and Tom for dinner at 7:30 p.m. The restaurant is about a fifteen-minute drive from your house so you agree that you should leave at 7:15 p.m. It all seems so simple. But here's what happens during those crucial moments before you leave the house.

5:45 to 6:30: Wife tries on fourteen different outfits, none of which she likes. When she asks her husband for help with deciding what to wear, he is faced with a problem, because all of the outfits pretty much look the same to him. So he picks one at random—number eight!—and the wife says that's her least favorite one and promptly sends the husband away.

7:01: Wife has settled on outfit number twelve, which she isn't crazy about, but she says it will have to do. It's unclear who she is talking to, because the husband isn't there. He's sitting on the couch, still in his gym clothes, watching the James Bond film *Live and Let Die*, which he's seen six times already.

7:02: Wife tells the husband they need to leave in thirteen minutes. Husband says he knows . . . and continues watching *Live and Let Die*, noting aloud that this is one of Roger Moore's best Bond films.

7:03 to 7:11: Wife reminds husband ten more times that they're leaving at 7:15.

7:12: Wife steps into the bathroom for thirty seconds to finish getting ready. When she pops her head out again, her husband is in the exact same position on the couch, only now he's wearing corduroy pants and a sweater. Husband tells the wife she needs to be ready to go in three minutes. Wife's head explodes.

7:15: Husband is waiting alone in the car.

7:21: Wife gets in the car, having changed outfits twice more. Husband starts to say something and wife turns to him and says, "Don't say a word." Husband pulls the car out of the driveway.

7:24: Husband pulls the car back into the driveway. Wife runs inside to get her wallet. And directions. And to pee.

7:29: You call your friends and tell them you might be five minutes late.

8:17: You arrive at the restaurant after stopping for gas, cash at an ATM, and directions (twice).

8:22: Kristen and Tom arrive at the restaurant.

By the way, if you're going to a movie instead of dinner, the timeline works much the same way, only it's much more stressful because the husband is worried about missing the previews, which, in his mind, would be about as bad as missing the birth of his child.

Sometimes the husband can be the source of the delay, although it usually involves extreme circumstances.

Reasons the Husband Could
Delay Departure from the House

1. There's two minutes left in the game.
2. Okay, now there's only, like, thirty seconds left in the game.
3. The game is going to overtime.
4. I need to call Steve real quick and talk about the game.
5. They're showing highlights of the game.

For the Husband

Guys, I have some bad news: part of being married is going out, on occasion, with people who your wife knows and you don't. For many guys this is as painful a realization as learning that the tooth fairy was really their mother (and that their mom still has the teeth in a box and shows them to houseguests).

There's nothing you can do about your mother (except maybe throw out the teeth next time you're home). But there is something you can do when your wife asks you to go out with some strangers: accept the offer. Resist the temptation to say, "I don't even know these people so why are we going out with them?" If your wife wants to have dinner with them then she obviously thinks you'll like them. So remember the lesson you learned way back in kindergarten: don't pass judgment on people before you've even met them (that's what the car ride home is for).

For the Wife

Ladies, if/when you do find yourselves acting as the social chair of your marriage, remember not to overdo it. A mature husband will go out with new people. But he'll also want to spend time with people you already know, or, better yet, just with you. Friday night at the movies with other couples is fun. But sometimes Friday night at the movies just the two of you is even better. And if, God forbid, you're going out on a Tuesday, there needs to be a really good reason, such as:

1. The two of you are having dinner with Beyoncé.
2. That's really the only acceptable reason.

14

Last Week, Were We Having a Debate about the Fabric Softener or the Dish Soap?

The Strange Tendency to Disagree about Past Disagreements

Back when the two of you were obnoxious teenagers, your parents warned you that someday you would grow up and be just like them. This, of course, was the most frightening threat that your parents could come up with, and it worked beautifully. You replied that you'd never be like them, slammed the door to your room, and dyed your hair magenta.

Now, all these years later, your parents are getting their revenge because their prophecy is coming true. Lots of couples have little disagreements. But only your parents ever had disagreements *about* their disagreements.

Your Mom: Steve, you were such a crybaby that time we were in Florence and I lost the key to the hotel room.
Your Dad: Damn it, Betsy, we were in London, not Florence!

And then, without warning, you have this conversation with your spouse:

Husband: Remember last time we came to this restaurant and you got all pissy because there was no parking?
Wife: No, I was pissy because the valet was too expensive.

Somewhere, your parents are laughing.

The fact of the matter is that disagreeing about past disagreements is a rite of passage. Some would say you're not truly married until you've forgotten the details of an event that's happened since you've been married. Other people would disagree with this statement, but I can't remember who they are.

Story Time

One particular type of disagreement about past disagreements seems to crop up most often: the retelling of a story to friends. The idea behind telling such a story is fairly straightforward—the two of you wish to entertain your friends by recounting an amusing anecdote about, say, your recent snorkeling mishaps or how difficult it is to understand people from Scotland ("They speak English, but you'd never know it! Am I right, people?!").

But the reality of telling such a story winds up being much different from what you intended. There's lots of ways things can go very wrong.

Storytelling Mishap 1: Who's the Narrator?

This is the classic storytelling problem: who gets to play narrator—the husband or the wife? The issue is usually still being debated after the storytelling has begun. Here's how it typically plays out:

1. Husband and wife have a six-minute debate about who should begin the story.
2. Coin toss decides it.
3. Wife begins under jealous glare of husband, who wishes he had won the coin toss.
4. Wife messes up an inconsequential detail of the story such as saying the temperature that day was in the low sixties, when, in fact, it was really the high fifties.

5. Husband pounces on the error and, without permission, starts telling story again from the beginning because "you're messing everything up."
6. Husband retells story and, in his haste to correct his wife's inconsequential error, omits a crucial detail like, "that's when we got arrested" or, "the hospital was out of penicillin."
7. Because husband's version of the story makes no sense, wife retells entire story in such alarming detail that the night ends while she is still only 7 percent of the way through the yarn.

Storytelling Mishap 2: Pulling the Plug

In this scenario one person actually tells the story correctly (a triumph!), but the spouse decides halfway through the story that it's a stupid tale because:

a. it's too embarrassing ("Why do you always tell the story where I come across as a moron?") *or*
b. it's too inappropriate ("Why are we discussing my breasts at the dinner table?") *or*
c. it's too boring ("Okay, so we overpaid in the taxi! Big deal! Who cares?")

Storytelling Mishap 3: Stealing the Thunder

To avoid (more) embarrassment, the two of you have decided ahead of time who the narrator will be. The other person is allowed to provide color commentary, albeit sparingly. But, inevitably, the color commentary doesn't enhance the story as much as it ruins it. As the wife is building up to the climactic scene at the Eiffel Tower, the husband says something like, "cut to the part where the guy falls off the tower!"

Storytelling Mishap 4: The Reluctant Story

Sometimes one of you hates the story before it even begins. But your spouse has set you up. And if you don't tell the story, he or she will do it for you:

Wife: Tell them the story about how you used to sleep with a blanket.
Husband: Oh, they won't find that interesting.
Wife: Sure they will. It's hilarious!
Husband: Let's just enjoy our food. This polenta is delicious!
Wife: So the blanket was named Shirley, and it was bright pink!

Storytelling Mishap 5: The Friends You Are Telling This Story to Have Already Heard It . . . Several Times

Not only have you forgotten the details of the story, you've also forgotten who you've told it to. Or, even worse, you forgot that the Murphys went on that trip to Paris with you and that it was their nephew who fell off the Eiffel Tower. (Don't worry—he survived and was given a lifetime supply of Brie for his troubles.)

No matter which mishap occurs, the result is always the same: your friends who were listening to the story quietly get up, leave the restaurant, and are never seen again. Afterward, you have this conversation:

Husband: [*visibly annoyed*] Great! There go the Murphys!
Wife: The same thing happened last summer when we told that story to the Bakers.
Husband: It wasn't last summer, it was only three months ago.
Wife: No, it wasn't.

Nuts and Bolts

Disagreements don't always center around long, involved stories (don't argue with me about that point). More often than not, you'll find yourselves disputing the facts about much more mundane incidents. The good news is that the Murphys aren't around to hear this banter. The bad news is that at least the Eiffel Tower story had a beginning, a middle, and, in theory, an end. But the day-to-day stuff is far more free-form.

Mundane Topic	He Says	She Says	Reality
Buying more coffee beans	"You always get the coffee beans."	"You started buying them during that weird phase when you only wanted beans that were 'shade grown,' whatever the hell that means."	Neither of you cares for coffee; you agreed several months ago to stop buying it altogether.
Writing post-Christmas thank-you notes	"I did it last year."	"You refused to use my proper pink stationery, so I did it."	You both sent notes last year, which is why you got double the pairs of socks this year.
Who left the open jar of oregano out on the counter	"You were the one making Italian food yesterday."	"No, I wasn't."	It's a jar of weed belonging to the plumber who was at your house yesterday. (He forgot it because he was high.)
Changing the water filter in your refrigerator	"I've never done that."	"Of course you did."	You bought a new fridge because husband couldn't figure out how to change the filter.
Birth control	"I thought you were still on the pill."	"Nope."	Wife is four months pregnant.

The important thing to remember is that there's actually something very romantic about the fact that the two of you can have such mundane disagreements.

Huh? Romantic?

That's right. Your spouse is the only person on the planet with whom you could possibly have a disagreement about the location of the ketchup because he or she is the only person on the planet who even cares where the ketchup is supposed to be. It takes a lot of intimacy to know these details. And intimacy is wonderful.

Now, many people are quick to point out that intimacy used to mean having sex twenty-three and a half hours a day. But that was back when you were nineteen, when you also thought that being "worldly" meant wearing a beret. So embrace the current ketchup intimacy in your life, because at least it doesn't involve a tiny, funny hat.

Storybook Ending

How do these little disagreements about past disagreements eventually resolve themselves? Like everything else in your relationship, the two of you have all the power. And by "the two of you" I mean "whichever one of you makes all the decisions."

You have the choice as to whether you want to drag these nagging disagreements on forever or get on with your life. Remember: you can always revisit this current disagreement down the road (and then disagree on what you were disagreeing about).

Since the two of you have the power of choice, the end of the disagreement will unfold much like a Choose-Your-Own-Adventure book.

Choose-Your-Own-Adventure Ending to Your Current Disagreement

Choice 1

The two of you look at your watches and realize you are quibbling because you are both tired and hungry. So you decide at once that it's time to . . .

a. Have a meal [Go to Choice 5]
b. Argue about what to eat [Go to Choice 2]

Choice 2

Two hours later, you decide on Indian takeout. While you're waiting for your food to arrive, you . . .

a. Kiss and make up [Go to Choice 5]
b. Fight about how the fight started [Go to Choice 4]

Choice 3

While you're debating who wanted to get Indian food, the dog sneaks up and eats all the takeout. You then spend the night at the vet because golden retrievers can't actually digest saag paneer. Better luck next time!

Choice 4

The food arrives and it is cold. But before you can say anything, the deliveryman just zips away. So you guys just . . .

a. Microwave the food [Go to Choice 5]
b. Try to remember whose idea it was to order from this place [Go to Choice 3]
c. Throw out the food and order something else [Go to Choice 2]

Choice 5

You did it! The argument is over! Enjoy your dinner of delicious Indian food (until one of you wishes you had gotten Chinese instead).

By the way, if you don't like the way your story played itself out, you can go back to the beginning and make different choices. Or you can just cheat and read all of the choices ahead of time and then plan your route (preferred method).

While these little disagreements usually resolve themselves quickly and painlessly, it would be even better, of course, if the two of you never had these disagreements in the first place.

No couple can eliminate all their squabbles, but here are some tried-and-true methods for keeping silly disagreements at an absolute minimum.

Solution 1: State the Obvious

The minute a silly dispute starts, just stop and point it out to each other. If saying "I think we're having one of those silly disagreements" sounds too self-aware, then come up with a code word you can say to each other to state the obvious. Just don't pick a word whose pronunciation you can't agree on, such as "potato," "tomato," or "nuclear."

Solution 2: Other Topics

If the two of you interject new topics of conversation into your life, it will make it easier not to relive any old debates. Go get a subscription to a serious magazine like *The Economist* and a fun magazine like *Us Weekly*. When the issues arrive, read them over. Then you can spend six seconds talking about monetary policy in Japan and fourteen hours talking about Gwyneth Paltrow's hair (which is way too long right now, right?).

Solution 3: Story Compromise

Best solution of them all! If you can't seem to agree on certain details of past events, just make up a version of what happened that you both enjoy. If one of you remembers the Ford Taurus rental car as being blue and the other one remembers it as being red, just compromise and say from now on that the Taurus was green. And while you're at it, instead of a Taurus, why not make it a Porsche?

Le Divorce

The thing that will really scare you straight, though, is when you learn that a couple whose wedding you went to is getting divorced. Even though there's that statistic that says that half of all marriages end in divorce, you never really think it will happen to any of your friends.

Moreover, the reasons your friends get divorced are never anything crazy, like the husband running off with a supermodel or the wife turning out to be gay and then stealing the supermodel from the husband.

Instead, when your friends confide in you about what went wrong, they say, "We were always fighting about little stuff, like the best place to park at the mall."

Upon hearing this news, the two of you break out in a cold sweat.

Husband: Oh, my God! We have disagreements all the time about where to park at the mall!
Wife: I know. You always insist on level five, which is too far away from the elevators.
Husband: But that's the whole point! There's plenty of spots over there!
Wife: We're doing it!
Husband: What?
Wife: Fighting about where to park at the mall! And we're not even at the mall right now. We're in our living room.
Husband: Are we going to get divorced?
Wife: No. I love you. I don't ever want to get divorced.
Husband: Me either.
[*Husband and wife have not-getting-divorced sex. Then, afterward:*]
Husband: Let's go to the mall.
Wife: Fine. But I'm driving.

Obviously, disagreeing about where to park at the mall doesn't mean you're getting divorced. The truth is that your friends had other issues in their marriage besides that.

But it's a cautionary tale nonetheless. The two of you appreciate that life is short. If you've found someone you love, why squabble with him or her? Agree that you'll never again fight about where to park at the mall. Or, at the very least, that you'll find a different mall with more parking.

For the Husband

Guys, I've managed to get all the way to chapter 14 before giving you this advice, but you had to know it was coming eventually. That's right—it's time to apologize!

When a silly disagreement happens, step up to the plate and apologize to your wife as soon as possible. You should do this *even if you're convinced that you were right*. Why? Because, at the end of the day, your argument is low-stakes. The disagreement wasn't about hostages in Iran or nuclear weapons in Cuba (at least, I hope it wasn't). So just be an adult and apologize for the way you stubbornly insisted it was Diet Coke, not regular Coke, that you spilled on your tie last month. It doesn't matter! Remember: you both agree that whatever was spilled completely ruined the tie she gave you for Valentine's Day. (By the way, you should probably apologize for that, too.)

For the Wife

Ladies, you need to resist the temptation to gossip with all of your friends about your husband's role in each of these tiny squabbles. There are several reasons for this.

First, these stories aren't very interesting. They may seem interesting to you, but they're not. The fact that you and your husband couldn't remember whether that Italian restaurant you liked in Dallas was called Lombardo's or Umberto's is not all that exciting. In fact, it's totally boring.

So seek your friends' counsel if your husband suddenly wants to move cross-country. But try not to be the girl who cries wolf every time your husband misplaces the car keys and asks you where you put them (even though it's perfectly obvious you didn't touch the keys and he knows it).

Also remember that your friends have their own husbands, which means they have their very own disagreements about past disagreements and don't need to live vicariously through yours. If your friends wanted to listen to a debate about whose mother supposedly said something insulting at last year's Thanksgiving dinner, they could have just stayed home.

15

What Are We Going to Do if There's No TV in the Hotel Room?

Planning a Romantic Weekend Away Together

One of the absolute best things you can do as a couple is find time to go away for a weekend trip just the two of you. It's the ultimate antidote after a tough stretch at work, an exhausting family reunion, or a nervous breakdown because you've called the plumber like fifteen times to fix the drain in the shower and he never called you back.

The first thing you need to decide is where the two of you should go. Needless to say, this is a most important decision. When you were first dating, a roadside motel would have been sufficient (because all you wanted was a place where your roommate wouldn't walk in and ask if you knew where the fabric softener was).

Now that you're married and living together, the situation is completely different. You've probably gone on a honeymoon, which was no doubt fabulous. A romantic weekend away doesn't have to be as elaborate as that trip, but after you've spent time at a nice resort, the motor lodge off the interstate no longer seems as romantic as it once did.

Here's the first rule on a romantic weekend getaway:

Try not to stay somewhere that is significantly crappier than your home.

You don't need to stay at the most expensive hotel. But you don't want to stay at a place that is significantly crappier than your own bedroom because there will be a zero percent chance of romance. Instead, you'll just have the following conversation again and again:

Husband:	I don't see why we're spending all this money to stay at this very crappy hotel.
Wife:	I agree.
Husband:	Do you want to have sex?
Wife:	No.
Husband:	Just a little bit?
Wife:	No.

At lot of people assume that there are exceptions to the Romantic Weekend Getaway Rule, but these are the same people who still think that a futon is comfortable to sleep on. Their logic should not be trusted.

Myth: It's okay to stay at a decidedly crappy place if it has an amazing view of the beach / mountains / St. Louis Arch.
Reality: Everyone enjoys a nice view of the St. Louis Arch. And about an hour later, you'd gladly trade that view if it meant having a shower in your room that actually made you feel cleaner when you used it.

Myth: It's okay to stay at a decidedly crappy place if it's really cheap.
Reality: Staying at home would be even cheaper, and there's no mysterious stain on the bedspread. (Your bedspread at home may be stained, mind you, but at least you know what caused it.)

Myth: It's okay to stay at a decidedly crappy place if you've been there before and it has sentimental meaning.
Reality: Remember when you were six years old and you thought Chuck E. Cheese's was the coolest place on Earth? Have you been back there as an adult? If so, you'll understand that sentimentality can be overrated sometimes.

Myth: It's okay to stay at a decidedly crappy place if you read a good review of it somewhere.
Reality: Yeah, I mean, college.dude.throwingup.blogspot.com has never done you wrong before.

Myth: It's okay to stay at a decidedly crappy place if that's the sort of place you like.
Reality: Only husbands believe this myth. No matter what your wife says, she would actually love to stay in a place where "free toilet paper!" doesn't need to be advertised as a perk.

If money is supertight and you're concerned that you may only be able to afford a place that is decidedly crappier than your home, then all you have to do is lower the water instead of raising the bridge. Translation: don't clean your bedroom for a while. Soon enough, your home will turn into such a complete disaster that *any* hotel will be less crappy than your home.

A Man, a Plan?

Now that you've established a minimum quality threshold for the weekend, the next obvious question is: who does the planning?

Your first instinct is that you should both do it together, but that's probably a terrible idea. Why? Because of the second rule of romantic weekends away:

Whichever one of you is the better planner
should be the person who plans the weekend.

Figuring out the planner among you is very easy. Just go and look at each other's closets. The odds are high that one of you has your shirts arranged by color and the other has his or her shirts arranged in a ball on the floor. The latter person is *not* the planner.

Now, many couples are uncomfortable with the idea that one person is doing all the planning. After all, the weekend is all about the two of you, so isn't it weird to have one of you doing all the work? Answer: no.

Think of it this way: if one of you is a five-star chef and the other can never figure out which side of the butter knife to use, who would you put in charge of cooking rack of lamb with black truffles?

You need to play to your strengths as a couple. Sharing is really awesome when you're messing around with Play-Doh in kindergarten. It's less awesome when you're adults and one of you is good at something and the other person sucks at it. So just let the more skilled person take the reins.

Inevitably, the planner will still have concerns about this strategy.

Concern	Reason It's Really Not That Big of a Deal
Won't the bad planner feel left out?	No. The bad planner hates planning.
That can't be true. Everyone loves planning!	No, *you* love planning. That's why you're the planner. Your spouse hates it and is thrilled to have you do it. That's one of the perks of being married to you.
But aren't we a team?	Look, Joe Montana was on a team, but that didn't mean he kicked the field goals.
Huh?	Sorry. Gratuitous sports analogy.
Well, shouldn't I give my spouse something to do? I mean, if I make the hotel reservation, maybe my spouse can find a restaurant.	Well, you can do this if you want, but your spouse will just pick the restaurant in the hotel. Then you'll get upset that your spouse didn't canvass the area for the best restaurant, which is what you would have done. In fact, you've already done it, haven't you? You couldn't resist.
Fine. I'll just plan the whole thing.	Good call.

Of course, the slim possibility remains that you both love to plan. If that's the case, you don't actually need to take the trip, because merely reading the guidebooks and getting hotel rate info makes you horny.

Location, Location, Location

With the decision-making hierarchy in place, it's time to narrow down the search of where to go. Here are some of the popular choices.

Winery Tour

Downside: you'll feel like a moron because you'll have no idea what the sommelier is talking about. Upside: you'll be drunk.

Las Vegas

Don't laugh. You may initially think of Vegas as a bachelor party destination, but Vegas also has great hotels, world-class restaurants, plenty of shopping, and tons of entertainment. The two of you will have a fabulous time . . . right up to the point when the husband says, "While you take a nap, I'm just going to play a little harmless roulette." As soon as he's out the door, the wife decides that she's not so tired after all and slips out to do a little browsing in the Forum Shops at Caesar's Palace. Two hours later, you're both broke.

Ski Weekend

Curl up by the fire together and have a mug of cocoa (after spraining your ankle and getting frostbite).

Nearby City

This can be a fun idea—hop in the car, drive a few hours to a neighboring city that you haven't explored before, and take in the sights together. However, after walking around the city for six minutes, you may realize that there's a reason you've never been there before.

Wilderness Lodge
Wow, honey, look—there's a brown bear! In our room!

Once you pick a destination, one of the real difficulties you'll face is finding a weekend when you are both free to go away. Even if you're not the most social people in the world, weekends have a way of filling up quickly.

For example, let's say you want to get away sometime in July or August. So you both look at your calendars and see the following:

Weekend	Conflicts
July 3–5	Bill Conlan's annual Fourth of July BBQ. You can't miss the sight of Bill endangering his life while trying to light fireworks.
July 10–12	Uncle Dave is in town on business and wants to treat you to a fancy expense-account dinner (translation: most important event of the summer).
July 17–19	Wife's company retreat; all employees go camping and spend weekend wondering why they're camping.
July 24–26	You have opera tickets that weekend because six months ago one of you freaked out and decided you needed more culture.
July 31–August 2	Alex Winchester and Wendy Prince are getting married that weekend in Palm Springs (daytime temperature: 153 degrees. Thanks, Alex).
August 7–9	Wife has appointment at the hair salon, which she had to make nine months ago.
August 14–16	Husband recovering from having wisdom teeth out.
August 21–23	Husband still recovering from having wisdom teeth out because he's a sissy.
August 28–30	Fantasy Football Draft (husband suddenly feeling much better).

Eventually, you guys decide to give the opera tickets away to some friends (you lie and tell them the tickets are for U2) and go away the weekend of July 24–26. You book two nights at a nearby spa and instantly get so excited that you tell everyone about your plans, including the cat, who reacts, as always, by violently scratching your cornea.

It's Go Time!

The spa weekend finally arrives and the two of you are very excited to spend some time together. Here's a timeline of how your romantic spa weekend may unfold:

Thursday Night

As the husband digs out suitcases from the depths of the hall closet, he pulls a muscle in his lower back. The good news is that he's getting a massage on Saturday. But now he needs $437 worth of Advil to get him through until then.

Meanwhile, the wife's boss is being a giant pain in the ass. Since she asked to leave at three o'clock on Friday, he's making her work late every day of the week until then. In fact, leaving three hours early on Friday has resulted in ten extra hours of work during the course of the week. The wife wants to ask her boss how in the world that's supposed to be fair, but the boss is at a spa getting a massage and is unavailable.

Friday Afternoon

Start to romantic weekend is delayed two hours as you search for car keys.

Friday Evening

The spa is about a two-hour drive from your house, which means you only get lost three times. One time it's the husband's fault, one time it's the wife's fault, and the third time you just start blaming the goddamn spa ("Couldn't they have just built it here—wherever the hell we are?!").

Friday Night

You finally arrive at the spa and, happily, find that it's as beautiful as you hoped. The husband is a little concerned that everything smells like lavender, even the men's room, but the wife assures him that it's okay to have your clothes smell like lavender if you're already married.

Your room is also lovely/lavendery and has a beautiful big bathtub. The two of you immediately decide to take a bath together. However, you discover that the tub is so large that it's virtually impossible to enter. The husband has to lift his wife into the tub, reaggravating his back muscle in the process. You stay in the tub for hours because, frankly, you're really scared about trying to get out.

Saturday Morning

You both wake up at six. The husband is way too hot because the duvet on the bed is much thicker than the one you have at home. Meanwhile, the wife is way too cold, because she left her flannel pajamas at home.

Saturday Midday

You go for a "nature walk," which involves walking the quarter-mile asphalt path from your room to the restaurant, where you stop and have lunch.

Saturday Afternoon

At long last, it's massage time. The husband is particularly excited because his back has now been hurting for two days. However, due to a mix-up at the spa, the husband is receiving the lavender aromatherapy massage that the wife is supposed to get. The therapist, who is Japanese and weighs about sixty-five pounds, kindly says she can switch to a deep-tissue massage. The husband agrees, not really believing this tiny masseuse can do all that much. And as he thinks that, the masseuse summons Herculean strength, which instantly reduces the husband to tears and meek cries of, "Not so hard, please!"

The wife, meanwhile, is in the room next door. She saw that the husband had an attractive Japanese masseuse, and now all she hears are his loud moans from his deep-tissue massage. The wife gets really stressed out listening to these moans, not quite sure what that Japanese masseuse is doing to her husband. The wife gets so stressed out, in fact, that she needs a second massage to recover from the stress of the first one.

Saturday Late Afternoon

The two of you enjoy the various spa facilities. The wife covers her body in twenty-eight different moisturizers, all of which smell like lavender.

The husband, meanwhile, spends two hours in the steam room, even though there is a sign that says it is extremely dangerous to go in there for more than ten minutes. But three other guys are in the steam room when he enters and it's instantly understood that they must all engage in a "steam-off" to see who can last the longest in the steam room without dying. The husband comes in second, but is later declared the winner when the guy who stayed in the longest has to go to the ER and is therefore disqualified. Well done, husband!

Saturday Evening

You enjoy a lovely, romantic dinner at the restaurant, sampling such spa menu favorites as lentil soup, lentil salad, and grilled salmon (with lentils).

You return to your room, excited for a night of lovemaking, and then instantly fall asleep from being so damn relaxed.

Sunday Morning

You check out and notice that the bill is five hundred dollars more than you thought it would be. This is because the wife got a facial and a manicure while the husband was in the steam room for two hours. The husband isn't upset, however, because he has another massage with the hot Japanese masseuse before breakfast.

Sunday Afternoon

You return home refreshed, relaxed, and very much in love . . . until you realize you left your wallet in the hotel room.

THE COMMON MISTAKE

Now, a word of caution.

Don't schedule the romantic getaway at the end of a different, not-in-any-way-romantic trip you're already taking.

It seems like such a good idea. You're already away . . . why not just turn that trip into a romantic one? Yes, these trips can work, but more often than not, they backfire severely.

Plan	Would Work If . . .	Won't Work Because . . .
Spouse joins you at end of business trip for a few nights of leisure.	. . . your business trip were to Maui.	. . . you're not in the pineapple, sugar, or macadamia nut business.
Take a vacation after attending a destination wedding.	. . . you're both excited to stay at the hotel where the wedding is taking place.	. . . the day after the wedding, the rate at the hotel goes up 952 percent.
After visiting your parents, spend a few days alone at their nearby lake house.	. . . lake house had indoor plumbing.	. . . parents have sold the lake house so your dad can fuel his midlife crisis and buy a motorcycle.
After testifying against your former mob bosses at a federal trial, stick around Washington, D.C., and see some sights.	. . . you were entering the witness protection program.	. . . city to which you'd be relocated has terrible Italian food.

When it's all said and done, remember that the most important part of any romantic weekend together is simply that the two of you get the chance to spend uninterrupted time together. Well, that, and the chance to use your Starwood points before they expire.

For the Husband

It's a nice idea to plan a little romantic surprise over the weekend for your wife: a bottle of champagne, a little present you brought for her, a nicer room than she was expecting (not hard since you booked the cheapest one).

And, for the record, inviting your friends along so you have a golf buddy is not a good surprise.

For the Wife

Although you don't want to go away with other people during your romantic weekend (see above), it's perfectly acceptable to ask your friends for recommendations. That way, you can avoid "scenic" hotels that face a landfill and "peaceful" hotels located next to an insane asylum.

In theory, your husband could do this, too, but that would involve having a conversation with his buddies about something other than whether beef or pork is the more awesome meat (such a hard call, right?). So it's probably best if you do the asking around.

16

What Do You Mean You Don't Like Paintball?

The Comedy That Ensues from Finding Common Interests

Every couple has activities that they enjoy doing together. After all, these common interests are probably part of the reason the two of you got together in the first place. Maybe you met while kayaking; perhaps you realized you had a mutual love of astronomy and went stargazing on your second date; or maybe you both just love to make out at the company Christmas party.

The problem is that you've managed to forget these common interests in the intervening months and years. This has happened because you were planning a wedding for the last eighteen months and now that it's over, you have absolutely no recollection of who you were and what you enjoyed doing before you became engaged. When people ask you what your hobbies are, you've gotten used to saying, "picking out appetizers, finalizing the guest list, and registering at Bloomingdale's."

But now that the wedding is over, the two of you must find ways to reconnect during your leisure time. One solution is to try to remember those activities that you did together when you were dating. With time, these memories should come back to you. If they don't, just make them up.

However, when you remember these activities, you may also recall that you didn't ever really enjoy them. The husband pretended he liked riding horses only because he thought it would make him look macho. Additionally, the wife now reveals that she really hates playing squash. She only played it back then because she thought it would help her membership application to the Midtown Athletic Club (which it didn't).

The reality, then, is that your interests and hobbies are constantly changing. Thus, husbands and wives need to keep each other updated about activities they want to do more of (photography) and less of (skydiving).

But before you figure out what activities you want to do with your spouse, you first must figure out what activities you yourself enjoy. In fact, you need to come to your spouse with a fairly long list so that when he or she shoots down 84 percent of them, you're still left with a few viable options.

Some folks have no problem sitting down and writing up a list of activities they enjoy. For example:

Activities I Enjoy

- Fishing
- Talking about fishing
- Cooking fish
- Visiting the aquarium
- Stealing fish from the aquarium and pretending I caught them

But sometimes making this list isn't so easy. Maybe the usual activities don't appeal to you; maybe you've lost a little sense of self over the years; or maybe you just don't have any paper.

In any event, for those who may be having a hard time, I've provided a handy template you can use.

Understanding Your Own Interests/Hobbies

Fill in each blank with an honest response.

After a hard week of work, the first thing I think about doing on Friday evening is: ______. Or, if that bar is too crowded, then I'll just go to ______ and get drunk with ______.

If the world were my oyster, I'd spend every Saturday morning ______. But since that's illegal, I'll be just as happy to ______, as long as ______ isn't going to be there, because he/she always ______, which makes me want to take his/her ______ and shove it into a ______ .

You can be damn sure, by the way, that I'll never ______ , and I don't care that your friend from college pays someone $ ______ to do that with them ______ times per week. Did you know you can get ______ from that? Seriously. I saw something on CNN about that.

The Activity Exchange Program

Now that you've each gotten to know yourself a bit better, one of the first things you'll decide to do is to have an activity exchange program. This exchange program involves the wife bringing the husband along to one of her favorite activities and the husband, in turn, bringing the wife along to one of his favorite activities.

The activity exchange program is full of good intentions, but, then again, so was the Vietnam War.

First, the wife brings her husband on a Saturday morning garden tour. The husband claims he is excited to get some sun and learn about geraniums. Four minutes into the tour, the husband has lost all interest in flowers and instead bides his time picking at a scab on his hand.

Later that day, in part two of the exchange, the husband takes his wife to a baseball game. The wife claims she is excited to get some sun and learn about the infield fly rule. Four minutes into the game the wife has lost all interest in baseball and instead bides her time trying to suture the scab on her husband's hand.

Thus, you both realize it's more fun to do these activities with your friends rather than your spouse. The activity exchange program ends as quickly as it began.

My Husband May Be a Moron

After the failure of the activity exchange program, the two of you may soon feel even more concerned about your common interests when you begin suffering from a mysterious syndrome:

My Husband May Be a Moron

Doctors at Harvard Medical School are still researching this condition, but here's a primer of what we know so far.

Typical Onset of "My Husband May Be a Moron" Syndrome

1. Wife recommends a book, documentary movie, magazine article, or other thought-provoking item to the husband.
2. Husband couldn't care less.
3. Wife gets totally freaked out that husband is showing no interest in this documentary she loved about the migratory habits of North American squirrels.
4. After weeks of nagging, husband finally agrees to watch documentary on squirrels.
5. Husband hates documentary.
6. Wife thinks husband may be a moron.

Suffice to say, this is a very serious condition. No husband wants his wife to think he's a moron (even if it's true). There are, thankfully, a couple of cures.

Potential Cures for "My Husband May Be a Moron" Syndrome

1. Husband pretends he actually likes the squirrel documentary.

2. When the wife figures out that her husband is lying about liking the documentary, the husband can make up an interesting-sounding reason why he didn't like it: "I thought they focused too much on black squirrels, which, frankly, are the least interesting variety."

3. When the wife still isn't convinced, husband watches documentary again and forces himself to like it.

4. Just when everything seems like it will be okay, husband then recommends a program for the wife to watch. The wife thinks the program is so dumb that she's once again convinced her husband is a moron.

In truth, the actual cure winds up being more of a tale of revenge. The husband feels bad about being a moron and so he offers to watch a different program with the wife—one that, ideally, doesn't involve squirrels.

Sensing an opportunity, the wife says she wants to watch the first episode of a new reality show involving a very girly activity like window treatments. The husband doesn't particularly care about window treatments, but after the first episode, he's hooked. So every Tuesday night, the husband runs to the TV, saying things like, "We have to find out if Chris's venetian blinds are going to get him kicked off this week!" The wife smiles to herself—her husband may be a moron, but at least that means he's easy to influence.

> Many men also wonder if there is a related condition called My Wife May Be a Moron. There isn't. And the fact that you thought there was only furthers the case that you may be kind of a moron.

Common Ground

You've weathered the awkward activity exchange program and (temporarily) cured My Husband May Be a Moron. And yet you're still back at square one: what activities can the two of us do together?

Not surprisingly, many people panic at this stage. In order to calm down, the best thing to do is to start simple. Not every common interest has to be complex or original. Consider some of these tried-and-true classics.

Sleeping

Not having sex, just simply . . . sleeping. It's something you both love to do for hours on end.

Eating

Did you have at least two meals yesterday, sweetie? Hey—me too!

Dealing with Stuff

This is a pretty broad category, which is good, because it means everyone can find some common ground here. This can be as grand as "we're both working to solve global warming" or as minute as "we both agree that the batteries in the remote control need to be changed."

Running Errands

A lot of couples derive pleasure from doing Saturday errands together. You're spending quality time with one another. And, more important, you're learning just how much money your spouse spends on dry cleaning, groceries, and random-ass knick-knacks that are going to get thrown out as soon as you get the chance.

Avoiding Phone Calls from Your Parents

Husband: Did you get the phone?
Wife: No, it was my mother. I didn't feel like talking to her. Did you call your mother back yet?
Husband: No.

Then, once you get your confidence up and realize that the two of you do, in fact, have a lot in common, you can start to push the envelope and take on new activities, such as:

Cooking Lessons

Everyone loves to eat, and cooking dinner together can be a great way for the two of you to catch up at the end of the day. However, after one of you slices her finger open and the other one burns his wrist, you can agree to order takeout every night for the next sixty years.

Museum Memberships

Many people assume that you should become a member of your city's museum only if you love oil paintings. But you should also join the museum if you're a lover of sculpture, antiques, architecture, or gift shops that sell twelve-dollar paper cubes.

The Cinema

What's better than taking in a classic movie or a fascinating foreign film during a Saturday matinee? The answer, of course, is the two-hundred-million-dollar romantic comedy that you eagerly rush off to see.

Bilingual Skills

In today's global economy, adding another language to your skill set will always be useful. So why not take some lessons together to make the process more fun? On the downside, you may soon turn into those annoying people who insist on speaking Italian when they order dinner, even though they're at an Olive Garden in Cleveland.

Travel the World

Put all your other skills to use! You now know about food, art, cinema, and language. So off you go to travel the world. When you return, you'll be more in love than ever. (And broke.)

You can also look to your friends for inspiration. After all, your buddies Gary and Shelly seem to have such a fun time together. They're always waking up at 7:00 a.m. on a Saturday to do some crazy activity. They've got to be on to something, right?

Wrong. Just because the activity is right for Gary and Shelly doesn't mean it's right for you . . . or anyone else, for that matter.

Odd Activity That Your Friends Seem to Enjoy	Version of Activity You Guys Enjoy
Waking up at dawn and digging for clams	Waking up at 10:27 a.m. and going to Starbucks
Training for triathlons by swimming for hours in the ocean	Sitting at a pool with lemonade (and every now and then trying to go in the water, but it's way too cold)
Gathering wild ferns and eating them	Gathering salad-in-a-bag from the grocery store at the corner
Building furniture	Sitting on your furniture (which you did not build)
Meditative breathing in the woods	Meditative breathing at Banana Republic
Tai chi	Thai takeout
Spelunking	Not spelunking

The only thing you've learned from doing these activities is that your friends Gary and Shelly are actually crazy people and should be viewed with caution from now on.

The Eternal Activity Dilemma

As the two of you sort through the many leisure activities available, you soon find yourself faced with the dilemma that confronts many couples:

Do I participate in an activity I sort of hate if it makes my spouse happy?

It's a curious debate. On one hand, you want to be loyal to your spouse. You want to show your husband, for example, that what he loves is inherently important to you. In essence, you need to show him that you'll do anything so long as you're together.

At the same time, though, you want to let your spouse know not to push his luck. Yes, you'll do anything with him—but do you really have to do it every weekend? Would it kill him to mix it up a bit and find something that isn't the most ridiculous hobby in the history of time? I mean, if you love someone, truly and deeply, shouldn't you feel safe telling him that bird-watching bores you to death (especially because you never seem to see any damn birds!)?

In truth, the answer as to whether you should be honest depends greatly on the activity in question.

Activity	Reason to Do It Even if You Hate It	Reason Not to Do It Even if Your Spouse Loves It
Hang gliding	It puts a smile on your spouse's face.	It puts a look of unbridled terror on your face.
Shopping for clothes	Everyone needs to update their wardrobe now and then.	When did "now and then" become "hourly"?
Sailing	Who doesn't enjoy a leisurely jaunt around the harbor?	Did you ever see *Dead Calm*?
Flea markets	There are a lot of diamonds in the rough out there.	No, there aren't.
Hunting	Might catch dinner.	Dinner might catch you.
Paintball	Safer than hunting.	Not really.

Eventually, you both realize that your favorite activity is to talk about all the stuff you want to do . . . and then hang around the house all weekend and do none of it. It's a classic pastime that's been bringing couples closer together for hundreds of years!

For the Husband

The best way to avoid the "My Husband May Be a Moron" syndrome is simply to listen to your wife when she recommends something she thinks you'll like. Remember that your wife knows you very well. Odds are high that she's telling you about something not just because she likes it, but also because she thinks you will too. So give her the benefit of the doubt. You'll never know just how interesting squirrels can be until you give them a try.

For example, did you know that all squirrels are mammals? See? How cool is that? Okay—it's not that cool. But watch the damn program anyway.

For the Wife

Ladies, you don't need to go over the top in your quest to find common activities. Sometimes a simple activity will do the trick. A Chinese food restaurant that you both love to frequent is sometimes just as effective a bonding experience as going bungee jumping together—and you're less likely to lose a limb eating kung pao chicken.

17

Now That We're All Settled In, We Should Probably Start Looking for a New Place, Right?

Battling the Inexplicable Desire to Continually Move

Part of the reason you get married is to have someone around to tell you when you're going insane. When the husband announces at 11:00 p.m. that he feels like making lasagna, the wife is there to tell him to go to bed. And when the wife is worried that everyone at a dinner party is going to notice a pimple on her back, the husband reminds her that she will (hopefully) be wearing clothes and that none of the guests has X-ray vision (that damn Clark Kent bailed at the last minute).

But what happens when you both go insane at the same time about the same thing? Who's there to tell you that you're acting crazy?

There are a couple of options, although you tend to dismiss these people's opinions very quickly.

People Who Tell You You're Acting Crazy	Reason You Dismiss Their Opinion
Your parents	That's the pot calling the kettle black, eh?
Your friends	Your friends rescinded the comment after you introduced them to a shortcut for getting to the movie theater.
Your dog	Is just as happy running in circles as he is giving you his opinion on your marriage.

Your therapist	Has been telling you for years that you're crazy. Talk about the therapist who cried wolf . . .
The little voices in your heads	If you were really crazy, the voices wouldn't tell you point-blank that you're crazy. Instead they'd tell you you were Joan of Arc and that you can talk to whales.

So, at the end of the day, there's really nobody around to tell you you're both going crazy.

Luckily, when the two of you go jointly insane, it's usually over benign topics.

- You both decide that your neighbor's cat is mean, even though all the cat did was look at you funny after you sat on him.
- You both decide that Dallas is too hot to live in, even though neither of you has ever been to Dallas.
- You both decide that the line at the Elm Street post office is about three minutes faster than the line at the Washington Street post office, so you only patronize the latter, even though it's an extra twenty minutes away.
- You both decide that the service at the Downtown Grill is terrible and you're never going back there again, although this is only because you showed up on a Friday night at eight without a reservation and they didn't have a booth available.
- You both decide that the car is making a funny noise, even though no other person on Earth can hear this noise.

On one occasion, though, when you both go insane at the same time, it spells serious trouble. You're sitting in your perfectly decorated living room, having a peaceful evening at home, when one of you turns to the other and says, "We should move."

There are, of course, some perfectly justifiable reasons to move, such as:

- Getting a new job in a new city
- Wanting to be closer to your family
- Needing more space
- Wanting to buy some real estate to diversify your portfolio
- You've just landed on Park Place, and your friend has a hotel there. You need to roll again and move as soon as possible.

But more often than not, the conversation about moving isn't fueled by one of these logical reasons. Instead, you have a strange desire to gravitate toward chaos in your life.

When you moved in together there was some chaos, but eventually it all got sorted out (read: thrown away). Then you got married, which brought with it more chaos in the form of wedding planning. But that, too, has passed, despite the fact the wife still likes to wear a tiara once a month. So now that the marriage commotion has subsided, everything is steady and good, just like you've always dreamed. One problem: you miss the chaos. You're addicted to the chaos. Where the hell is the damn chaos?!

Naturally, moving isn't the only form of chaos out there. You will consider alternatives, but it's likely you'll also systematically shoot them all down.

Alternate Form of Chaos	Reason It Gets Shot Down
Have kids	Too chaotic
Change careers	Too annoying
Take up a complicated hobby, like windsurfing or heli-skiing	Too midlife crisis
Hike the Appalachian Trail	Too cold
Have an open marriage	Too 1970s
Go get drunk in Spain and/or France	Too Ernest Hemingway

The fact is that moving provides the perfect outlet for chaos. It's something you were going to do in the future anyway (unlike windsurfing), so you're simply adjusting the timetable. And besides, at the end of the chaos you have something positive—a brand-new home—whereas at the end of windsurfing you have three thousand dollars in medical bills and a vague memory of surfing rapidly toward a rock.

The Origin of the Craziness

The process starts simply enough. You agree that you're just going to do some looking around on the weekends. You'll visit some open houses and get a sense of the market. You figure that, if nothing else, it's a great way to spend time together. Plus it's an excuse not to do more mundane tasks like figuring out where you're going to put the three gallons of peanut oil you deep-fried your Thanksgiving turkey in ("Will it kill the grass if we dump it in the yard?").

You start off acting very responsibly. Your goal is only to move up one rung on the housing ladder.

If you currently . . .	Then the logical next step is to . . .
Rent a small place	Rent a larger place
Rent a large place	Own a small place
Own a small place	Own a bigger place
Own a big place	Own a house that has the rooms featured in the board game Clue
Live with your parents	Cry

When you start looking around at places that are one rung up the housing ladder, you quickly realize that these places all kind of suck. They usually look a lot like the place you're already living in except that they have 5 percent more space for about 700 percent more money. Or, alternatively, the place looks great, but there's something hideously wrong with it, like:

- Needs all new wiring and plumbing
- Massive termite infestation
- Located next to an airport
- Located on an Indian burial ground

Suffice to say, none of the places that are one rung up the ladder are very appealing. So you quickly come to the conclusion that you should stay where you are because your current home is actually a really good deal.

Just kidding.

Instead, you start looking at places that are three or four rungs up the ladder. That's right—even though you're currently renting a one-bedroom apartment, you decide to go to open houses for five- and six-bedroom homes. These homes are all very lovely and would suit your needs quite nicely. Even the ones that are located on ancient Indian burial grounds are so large that only half the house is likely to be haunted.

You rush home and immediately start going through your finances to see if you can make the numbers work. This is, of course, a futile exercise. It's like wondering if three almonds is enough food for a dinner party involving twenty people. But through the magic of accounting, you come up with a formula that, in your minds, works.

The basic idea is that you:

- Sell everything you own.
- Go without food or drink or cars or clothes for ten years.

You ask your parents what they think of your plan and, appropriately, they tell you you're crazy. This is exactly what you wanted to hear because you're still immature enough to do the opposite of whatever your parents say. This strategy is, admittedly, getting tougher; in recent years you've had to come out in favor of famine just to take a stand against your parents.

However, your parents are not alone on this one. Your Realtor, your accountant, your boss, your friends, your siblings, your pets—they all think this is a terrible idea. In fact, the only person who comes out in favor of it is a friend of the husband's from college named Stu, whose occupation is currently a "freelance spiritual adviser." (Last week, Stu was a "journey enabler," which is to say he worked at Hertz Rent A Car.)

Stu tells you that you both must walk down a path together if you are to communicate with trees. You have no idea what this means, and it's worth noting that Stu is high when he tells you this. Nonetheless, Stu is just the enabler you need.

You get set to make an offer on the house, elated with the chaos that is bound to ensue! And then your heart breaks. Some other couple has already made an offer on the house, and the seller has accepted it. Apparently this other couple had a few things going for them as buyers, such as the ability to actually pay for the house.

You then quickly spiral out of control and start putting offers on dozens of homes, including ones you don't like and haven't seen. Somehow you keep getting outbid, even though the real estate market is slowing and you should have an advantage. The Realtor tells you that you could use a cooling-off period, so you immediately fire her. But since the word on the street is that you're crazy, no other Realtor will take you on.

You have no choice but to sulk home to your abode, which now seems tinier than ever. You've been saved from financial ruin. Your life is *not* in complete chaos. Can it get any worse?!

The Real Insanity

Up until this point, the two of you have been acting irrational and crazy, but you've done so as a team. Fun! But now that you've been given a momentary reprieve from the insanity, your paths will suddenly split. One of you will come to your senses and realize that moving—especially to a place you can't afford—is a foolish pursuit. The other will continue deeper into insanity and insist that the time is right to start looking at seven-, eight-, and even nine-bedroom houses.

Either of you could play the role of the crazy person. It has nothing to do with gender or age or zodiac sign. It's just random chance, like being called for jury duty. But you'll soon find yourselves having this conversation:

Rational Spouse:	Look, let's put this whole moving thing on hold for a while.
Insane Spouse:	You mean like for a few minutes? Do you have to go to the bathroom?
Rational Spouse:	No. I mean, yes, I do kind of have to go to the bathroom, but that wasn't what I meant. Let's save up some money for a few years before we buy a house.
Insane Spouse:	Why?
Rational Spouse:	Well, do we really need an eight-bedroom house?
Insane Spouse:	Yes. A master bedroom, a guest bedroom, a bedroom for each of our two kids, an office for each of us, and a room for the pandas.
Rational Spouse:	We don't have any pandas. Or children. And that's only seven bedrooms anyway.
Insane Spouse:	You're right. We really need ten bedrooms.

The rational spouse needs to act fast. It's his or her responsibility to bring the insane spouse back from the edge, and to do so before you own pandas. Yes, it's a burden, but your spouse will do the same for you someday, when you go through your phase of thinking that it's a good idea to buy a farm and make artisanal cheeses.

You can use a couple of different solutions to rescue your wayward spouse.

Change Something Else in Your Life

This is sort of like giving smokers that nicotine gum: it's still bad for them, but at least it's not as harmful as what they were doing before. So instead of buying a new home you don't really need, maybe you should just go get some shoes and maybe a frying pan that you don't really need.

Watch Some Discovery Channel Documentary about Domestic Dangers

Once your spouse learns about how radon gas can leak up from your basement and poison you, he'll be too scared to move. Hopefully it will never occur to your spouse that these domestic dangers could, of course, be happening in your current home as well.

Watch The Money Pit *Starring Tom Hanks and Shelley Long*

Everybody loves those Tom Hanks comedies from the eighties. And even if you don't love slapstick, it's still funnier than that Discovery Channel show on radon gas—whose idea was it to watch that?!

Rearrange Stuff in Your Current Home

This works surprisingly well. If you switch which kitchen cabinets contain the glasses and the plates, the resulting confusion could distract your spouse for weeks or years.

In the end, the irrational urge to move winds up being just a passing fad. So the best solution is simply to wait it out. Your spouse will soon move on to other irrational ideas, like changing hair color or learning to play the tambourine. These are equally as crazy as moving, but at least they don't involve escrow.

For the Husband

If your wife's desire to move is more than just a passing fad, you can suggest redecorating your existing place.

The truth is that your wife may want to move because she's feeling bored with your existing rooms. A little redecorating will fix that and thus extend how long she'll feel content in your current home.

To be sure, redecorating can be a pain. For example, if you're painting the bedroom a new color, you need to:

- Decide on a color
- Change your mind about the color a minimum of ten times
- Get the paint
- Change your mind about the color three more times
- Move all the furniture out of the room
- Paint the walls
- Move all the furniture back into the room
- Realize you've done a terrible job
- Hire a professional painter to redo the work

Men, here's one cautionary word of advice: once the redecorating machine starts, it's very hard to turn it off. After you're done redoing the living room, then it's on to the bedroom, bathroom, kitchen, dining room, den, hall closet, backyard, and attic. And once you're done with those rooms it will be time to start over with the living room again.

Redecorating also costs money. In fact, some sofas are more expensive than, say, a Volvo. But redecorating will definitely be cheaper and easier than moving.

Plus, if you buy a new couch, you'll have it for a long time. If you do decide to move someday, the couch can come with you. In fact, for what that couch cost, it's not only going to be in every home you ever live in, but it's also coming to important life events like weddings and graduations.

For the Wife

I, myself, am a man, and I don't want to reduce my gender to a bunch of simpletons, but, that said, let me offer the following advice: if your husband is going through a bout of temporary insanity, it's probably just because he's hungry.

As a woman, you will find this explanation hard to believe, for two reasons:

1. He just ate, like, two hours ago.
2. Are you really telling me that there's a link between a guy getting hungry and inexplicably wanting to move to a twenty-three-bedroom house?

The responses to these concerns are quite simple:

1. So?
2. Yes.

Let's start with the first one. How recently your husband has eaten is an irrelevant stat, as is what he ate. Even though he had a twenty-three-thousand-calorie chicken parmesan sub two hours ago, he could still be hungry. In fact, he's probably starving because his stomach has expanded to the size of a small pony.

And hunger will most certainly turn your husband into a crazy person. He will announce that he wants to run for Senate. He will decide that Thanksgiving should really be held in July. He will bark at the dog for hours.

Do not be alarmed. All he needs is a turkey sandwich. And some chips. And maybe a Diet Coke. Minutes after he's eaten, he'll withdraw from the Senate race, reaffirm Thanksgiving's location in late November, and once again speak English to the dog (who still can't understand what he's saying anyway).

Most important, he won't want to move. And by that I mean he physically won't want to get off the couch.

18

Don't We Have a Constitutional Right to Stare at Attractive People (Even if We're Not Married to Them)?

What Happens When You Check Out Someone Who Is Not Your Spouse

When one of you comments on the attractiveness of someone besides the other of you, problems may ensue. One school of thought says you have agreed to be attracted to one person forever. Therefore, any comments about the beauty of someone else are always going to be hurtful to your spouse and you should avoid them.

A second school of thought suggests that being secure in your marriage means that you can compliment other people without making your spouse feel threatened.

And, for the record, there's also a third school of thought: when a man checks out another woman, he's showing an appreciation for female sexuality, which, in turn, proves he is a great lover. This school of thought, incidentally, is held only by men.

And So It Begins . . .

Since, by definition, most wives tend to be women, they are probably well aware that men have a very hard time ignoring women's breasts. Now that he's married, of course, a husband will do his best to suppress his gazing at all women except for his wife. But, just like a comet, the habit continually returns.

One of the most common ways in which this occurs is at a restaurant. The husband and wife will be seated at a table having a lovely dinner for two. And then, right in the middle of an interesting conversation about whether Uncle Mel has grown another chin, the husband inadvertently stares at an attractive woman who happens to be passing by the table on her way to the ladies' room. It's just a subtle move of his eyes, but his wife notices this 0.000342-millimeter shift in his pupils.

The wife's first reaction is to be annoyed. But she also realizes that she has caught her husband in a reflex reaction. It's like getting mad at him because his leg jerks when a doctor hits his knee with a rubber hammer.

The wife's second reaction is to try to use the situation to her benefit. So the wife waits until the woman returns from the bathroom. The wife now gets a good look at this other woman's breasts and says, under her breath, "If those aren't fake, they should be in a museum." The wife pretends she can't believe what she just said, the husband starts laughing, and the husband's thoughts are now back on the awesomeness of his wife. He forgets all about that other woman and her breasts (until she goes to the bathroom again).

Unfortunately, not all comments and/or behavior from husbands wind up being as benign as a subtle shift of the eyes.

To help wives know whether their husband's behavior is common or something to worry about, I've provided the following scale:

Danger Level 1 (Least Severe):

Husband is excited because he has arranged for the *Sports Illustrated* swimsuit issue to be delivered to the house.

Danger Level 2 (Still No Big Deal):

Husband is antisocial for a few hours after the *Sports Illustrated* swimsuit issue arrives.

Danger Level 3 (A Little Odd):

Husband tells his wife that he thinks she should buy one of the swimsuits featured on the magazine, even though the swimsuit he's referring to is actually just body paint (and, inexplicably, still costs $575).

Danger Level 4 (Starting to Get Really Weird):

Husband builds special oxygen chamber to keep pages of swimsuit issue from deteriorating.

Danger Level 5 (Hmmm . . .):

Husband and swimsuit issue take a romantic trip away together, just the two of them.

The Other Foot

Many men are surprised to learn that their wives also check out other people. But unlike their husbands, wives tend to be enchanted with other traits in addition to physical appearance. When husbands discover this fact, they get defensive and try to convince their wives that they already have these traits, so there's no need for her to be checking out other men. This process usually backfires drastically.

Trait	What Wife Says about Other Guy Who Has This Trait	Husband's Desperate Reaction to This News
Sense of humor	"Steve has such a quick wit! He always makes me laugh!"	Tells wife deeply offensive joke.
Handy around the house	"The electrician put dimmers on every switch in the house in under ten minutes."	Awkwardly inserts the phrase "Phillips-head screwdriver" into every conversation.

Kindness	"That sweet guy from the mail room wished me a happy birthday today."	Wishes wife happy birthday on days that aren't her birthday.
Intelligence	"Ted is easily one of the smartest people I've ever met."	Tells wife that he is ten times intelligenter than Ted.
Reliability	"This client said he was going to call me back within ten minutes and he did. How refreshing is that?"	Husband says he's also going to call his wife back within ten minutes . . . which is odd, because he says this as they're lying in bed together.
Plays an instrument	"Have you ever heard Mike play the piano? It's beautiful."	Buys piano. Plays "Heart and Soul" on continuous loop.

To be fair, though, wives will still comment on the physical attributes of other men as well. Remembering how understanding his wife was when he accidentally stared at a stranger's breasts, the husband tries to return the favor when he catches his wife staring at another guy's ass. Stealing the wife's line, the husband says, "If that ass is real, it should be in a museum!"

The awkward silence that follows lasts several months.

Reversal of Fortune

The golden rule of life is that you should do unto others as you would have them do unto you. I have no idea what the silver and bronze rules are, although my guess is they probably have something to do with how long you have to arrive at the airport before an international flight and/or why the phone company can't give you anything smaller than an eight-hour window during which they may show up to fix your jack.

Anyway, back to the golden rule. It can also apply to checking other people out. That is, if you're going to do it, be prepared for it to happen to you as well.

The awkward situation that occurs isn't so much when someone pays you a compliment—who doesn't like that?—but rather it's when you overhear a comment about your spouse. There's a very fine line between a kind compliment and a creepy one. And things can go bad instantly.

Stage 1: The Discovery

This is where you discover that a coworker or friend has said something about (or stared at) your spouse. The most obvious way this happens is when it's done directly in front of you. This may seem like the most awkward situation ("Um, dude, I can see you looking at my wife's chest!"), but, in truth, most people will generally use tact and censorship in your presence.

Far more dangerous is when you hear about comments through the grapevine. Comments made to a third party tend to be a lot more liberal—"I bet Len's wife is a monster in bed!"—and, even worse, lots of people have now heard the comment and are thinking about it. Thus, when you go to get your morning coffee in the office break room, all your friends are staring at you and wondering (a) if you had sex with your wife last night and (b) whether it was as good as they think it was.

Worst of all is when the comment is made publicly, such as in a wedding toast, on an Internet blog, or at halftime of the Super Bowl.

Stage 2: The Comment

The actual comment made is, of course, a key variable. Everyone reacts differently, but here are some examples to illustrate the very fine line between classy and creepy.

Classy Comment about Your Spouse	Creepy Comment about Your Spouse
"Laura is so elegant."	"Laura has a wonderfully rare combination of classic elegance mixed with pure, raw hotness."
"Ben has a fabulous head of hair."	"I found a strand of Ben's fabulous hair on the floor. May I keep it?"
"Wendy seems very fit and athletic."	"Do you think Wendy's strong enough to pin me down?"
"Your husband has very distinctive eyes."	"I always feel like your husband is undressing me with those distinctive eyes of his. But in a good way. A very good way."
"Your husband looks like a mountain man when he hasn't shaved in a couple of days."	"That beard is ticklish when it rubs against your skin."
"What's the name of that perfume you're wearing, Alison?"	"It's Chanel, right? Here—I bought you a bottle."

Stage 3: The Reaction

This is your chance to fight creepiness with . . . more creepiness. Guys tend to react one of two ways when they overhear a comment about their wife. The first, and more traditional, reaction is to angrily ask the guy who made the comment if he's having an affair with the wife.

The second, and more unsettling reaction, is to encourage more inappropriate comments. Some men have married very hot women with the hope that their friends will make comments about her beauty so that he'll feel all the more awesome for having married her. But these guys' enthusiasm for hearing creepy comments is, in and of itself, very creepy.

Women, on the other hand, tend to take compliments about their husband with a more even keel. If a comment is odd, they'll politely let it pass. If a comment is appropriate and generous, they'll agree. And if a comment is really inappropriate, they'll announce angrily that if anyone messes with their man, there'll be hell to pay (but they say that with an even keel).

Stage 4: The Discussion

Once the comment has been made, the hardest part is recapping the situation for your spouse. You're not worried that your spouse will be upset—because, again, everyone likes hearing a compliment about himself or herself.

Rather, the struggle comes from the inevitable high-and-mighty attitude your spouse will have. For the next week, your spouse will prance around the house saying things like, "Gary likes my legs," or, "Your friend Sarah would have laughed at that joke because she thinks I'm charming."

Stage 5: The Repeat

There are really two versions of the repeat. One is where the same man who made the first comment about your wife makes a second comment. At this point, it's perfectly acceptable to tell this person to keep his mouth shut. You let the comment about your wife's eyes slide. But now that he's making another comment about her raw sexuality, a line has been crossed. You can either tell him point-blank to stop or you can fight fire with fire and make a creepy comment about *his* spouse. Although, most of the people making creepy comments tend not to have spouses.

Husband: You know what, Bob, your wife has a great ass.
Bob: I'm not married.
Husband: Well, then, someday you're going to marry a woman with a great ass.
Bob: Um . . . thanks. That sounds great.

Husband: [*disappointed*] Yeah, it does. It was supposed to be creepy but it came off as a compliment. Damn.

Bob: Will my wife's ass be as great as your wife's ass?

Husband: Why are you so good at being creepy, Bob, and I'm struggling with it?

Bob: Probably because you're a kind soul with soft skin and gentle eyes.

Husband: You just did it again, Bob! That was an incredibly creepy comment! I need to go take a shower and wash your creepiness away.

The second type of repeat happens when a totally different person makes the exact same comment about your spouse that someone else did. In this case, it's hard to be upset. If two strangers both say that your husband has a good body, well, then he probably does. Either that, or your husband has paid these women to say that about him.

For the Husband

Men, here's a reminder that you should tattoo onto your cerebellum: always find the time to compliment your wife more than anyone else. If your wife is looking very beautiful one night, tell her. Yeah, she's heard it before, but it always means a lot when it comes from you.

Compliments and flowers aren't just for when there's a bump in the road. They also work well when you give them for no reason whatsoever other than the fact that you want to.

Besides, your wife is realistic. She knows that you have testosterone pumping through your body and, as a result, will find it hard to walk down a beach without a little staring. Fine. But if you find the time to make your wife the object of your affection, it lets her know that any gazing around is benign, and not a sign that you need to be monitored 24/7 by a group of elite female CIA agents. Although that sounds kind of hot, right?

For the Wife

Women, you don't have to agree with something just because all your friends do. Your pal Stephanie may laugh about how her husband is always commenting on other women's breasts. But if your husband does the same thing and it annoys the crap out of you, say something to him about it.

You're not Stephanie and you don't have to live by her (annoying) rules. And if your husband pulls out the "Well, Stephanie thinks it's funny" line, remind him that Stephanie is on her third husband and she's mean to puppies and you're never speaking of her again.

19

Does the Company Softball Game Count as Quality Time Together?

The Eternal Struggle to Balance Your Career with Your Marriage

There are 168 hours in a week (that's a fact, by the way, not my opinion). Sometimes, it seems like there just aren't enough hours to devote to your spouse. Our jobs, in particular, consume much of our time. Consider that most people spend:

- Forty hours a week working at their job
- Five hours a week getting ready to go to their job
- Five hours a week commuting to their job
- Fifty hours a week sleeping so that we're able to do our job well
- Ten hours a week "vegging out" after we get home from our job

When you add it all up, that's 110 hours. Which means you only have fifty-eight waking hours to spend with your spouse.

Fifty-eight waking hours? Every week? That sounds like an eternity! What the hell is the problem, exactly?

I'll Be Home Somewhere between Seven and Midnight

Naturally, even with the fifty-eight (*fifty-eight!*) waking hours together, there are still many times when your job gets in the way of your marriage. One of the most common is when one of you gets stuck working late at the office.

If you know ahead of time that one of you will be working deep into the night, it's an annoyance, but not a total disaster because at least you can plan ahead. The spouse stuck at the office gets treated to dinner courtesy of the company, although an unofficial rule holds that this meal must, weirdly, consist of at least fourteen thousand calories, so all the coworkers debate whether to have Chinese food or pizza. When someone suggests getting salads, that person is immediately fired.

The spouse at home has the evening to himself or herself. The wife, let's say, tells her husband that she's just going to have a quiet evening at home . . . and then she goes to the movies and dinner with eight friends and has the most awesome night ever.

The husband is glad that both of your nights weren't ruined, but a tiny part of his brain is freaked out about how little he was missed. Next time he gets stuck at work, the husband insists on conference calling into the evening.

The bigger problem is when one of you has to work late unexpectedly. This can wreak havoc on your social life in many different ways.

Scenario 1: You Have Plans to Go Out

With one spouse stuck at the office, the other spouse faces a dilemma: cancel the plans or go alone. If you cancel plans at the last minute, then you're one of those annoying friends who is always canceling plans at the eleventh hour. If you go without your spouse, then the night can be socially awkward as you apologize profusely for having to come alone. And, inevitably, your plans are with people who know your spouse better than they know you, so you have to spend the evening going through this annoying conversation:

Them: Tell us about yourself!

You: Well, I'm an architect. Actually, I'm studying to be an architect. I'm still in grad school.

Them: What else?
You: I'm an avid jogger. I'm running my first marathon in two months.
Them: What else?
You: When I was ten, I won the National Spelling Bee.
Them: What else?
You: I have gills.
Them: What else?
You: Are you even listening to my answers? I just told you I had gills. Which, were it actually true, should be the most amazing thing you've ever heard.
Them: What else?

Scenario 2: You Have Plans Just the Two of You

This is an even tougher situation. Blowing off friends because you have to work is frustrating. But having to cancel on your spouse really makes you upset. Yes, your spouse understands ("We can celebrate Valentine's Day in March, along with all the other lawyers . . ."), but your guilt runs deep. So you tell your boss that you're not having enough family time, and your boss says he totally understands and suggests getting a divorce—that way, no conflict. You decide then and there that you're going to quit your job and open a restaurant. You do, and then, three months later, after the restaurant fails, you go back to the law firm.

Scenario 3: You Have No Plans

This seems as if it would be the easiest scenario to deal with—after all, you don't have any plans. But the problem is more for the spouse who remains at home alone. There's not really enough time to plan anything, so he or she has dinner alone and watches TV. No big deal . . . the first ten times it happens.

But eventually the spouse at home starts to go totally insane without the other person there to keep him or her company. Indeed, you come home from work one night and realize your spouse has started giving the furniture names and referring to it as "my friends."

If you're both stuck working late, then you definitely have to cancel whatever social plans you had that night (no sushi with Bob and Lisa tonight). You both roll into the house at, like, 10:00 p.m., too tired and exhausted to say anything to each other. The wife has a glass of wine while the husband takes a bath. And then you suddenly realize that you both enjoy those activities more than sushi with Bob and Lisa.

And if neither of you is working late, you're both secretly wondering if the other person should be working just a little bit harder.

On the Road Again

Business travel is another challenge on the work/social seesaw. Quality time together instantly vanishes because one of you is home alone while the other is at a soulless hotel near an airport.

For the person on the road—let's say it's the wife—her usual evening routine is replaced with activities that don't really seem to measure up.

Normal Evening Activity	Business Travel Evening Activity
Walking the dog	Listening to the dog barking in the next hotel room
Watching favorite TV show	Spending forty-five minutes trying to figure out how to use the hotel remote control
Talking to spouse about upcoming weekend plans	Talking to coworkers on the least important topics ever discussed, such as the pros and cons of the new coffee machine in the office kitchen

Taking a hot bath	Taking three hot baths because this business trip is in Minneapolis in the middle of friggin' January
Devouring a chapter or two of a good book	Reading over the next morning's PowerPoint presentation for the 3,290th time

To combat the hotel blues, the wife on the road checks in with her husband each night, but those conversations never seem to be very satisfying.

Spouse at Home: Hey, how was the meeting?
Spouse on the Road: Great. The client really liked the presentation.
Spouse at Home: Cool.
Spouse on the Road: What are you doing tonight?
Spouse at Home: I got a microwave pizza. And there's a dog show on NBC I want to watch. How about you?
Spouse on the Road: I got fettuccine Alfredo from room service but it was kind of congealed by the time it got here.
Spouse at Home: Cool.
Spouse on the Road: Miss you.
[*Conversation is repeated verbatim every night of business trip.*]

The good news is that the spouse at home took the time to do some chores that he otherwise never seemed to get around to, like hanging pictures. Just kidding. He actually just watched TV every night and, thus, that piece of art you got last summer is still sitting on the hallway floor.

The spouse who was away on the trip wants to say something, but she knows that she'll be home alone next week and she will really just want to watch TV for three days as well and not have to do any damn chores either.

One solution to the business trip blues is to bring back a little present for your spouse every time you go away. It shows that you're always thinking of him. And because he loves you back, he hasn't told you that a collection of magnets that says things like, "Hello from Houston!" and "Greetings from Green Bay!" is a pretty lame gift. I mean, how could you go to Wisconsin and not bring back a wheel of cheddar?!

Socializing with Strangers

Even tougher than business travel are the dreaded company social events. Few things are more painful than being dragged by your spouse to the company softball game or to Jim Wainwright's retirement party or to the CFO's annual cookout ("It's a write-off!").

The problem with these events, of course, is that your spouse knows everyone and you don't. Yes, you've met all the coworkers before, but it's not anywhere close to spending ten hours a day with them, which is what your spouse does. The day holds many notable moments for you.

Highlights of Your Spouse's Company Social Event

- Trying to stay awake while your spouse's boss tells you way too much information about the business ("Gosh, Ned, I didn't know that MediaTek did over $1.4 million in sales last year in Paraguay. That is fascinating.")
- Explaining what you do no less than four hundred times ("I manage the restaurant, which is different from being the chef, so please don't ask me again if I know how to cook a leg of lamb.")
- Listening to your spouse make lots of inside jokes with his or her coworkers, including comments like, "You'll never have

hot sauce again, huh?" and "You write the best memos in the office, if you know what I mean!"
- Bonding with other spouses about how bored you all are.
- Begging your own spouse to take you home.

The good news is that you can usually eat as much as you want at events like this. Your spouse may have to work the room a bit (with you in tow, as though you were on a leash) but eventually you'll be set free and can dig in. Who ate the last piece of key lime pie? You did. And you're pretty damn pleased about it.

By far, though, the most dreaded moment of any company social event is:

- Learning, to your horror, that your spouse has discussed way too much about your personal life with her or her colleagues.

So, as if the office Christmas party wasn't bad enough, someone now comes up to you and says, "I hear you're having a fight about where to spend New Year's Eve." Swell.

So you get home, totally annoyed at your spouse. She apologizes profusely and explains that she didn't mean to reveal this private information, but she got trapped. Her boss walked into the office and asked, "What's up?" and she needed a better answer than, "I'm playing solitaire on my computer, that's what's up."

You quickly forgive your spouse because you love her. Also, your office Christmas party is next week. (And, um, you may have said something to your coworkers about your spouse's foot fungus.)

Bad Day at the Office

Office parties happen once, maybe twice, a year. However, a bad week at the office can happen anytime. When a bad work week strikes, spouses will do whatever they can to make your week a bit easier—a glass of wine, a back rub, and/or a fight to the death with your boss.

Sometimes, though, despite their best efforts to be a calming influence, spouses can't help but nag you about certain things. Yes, you had to work late on the presentation, but your spouse points out that you still have to figure out what day you want to fly to Chicago for Thanksgiving because the airfares are going up exponentially by the hour. You get a little annoyed with your spouse ("I don't care when we go to Chicago! Pick a damn day!"), but at least you understand where he or she is coming from.

But sometimes spouses can cross the line with their urgent requests and nag you about stuff that couldn't be more stupid or irrelevant. Normally you can handle it, but this week—forget it.

Annoying Question You Can Ask Even When Your Spouse Is Having a Bad Week at Work	Annoying Question to Avoid When Your Spouse Is Having a Bad Week at Work
Do you care what day next week the guy comes to paint the bedroom sky blue?	Is sky blue a primary color?
Will you please say hello to my mother on the phone? It's her birthday.	Will you talk to my mother at length about the mediocre Caesar salad she had at lunch?
Can you please sign our tax return so we can file it before the deadline?	What percentage of Americans do you think sign their tax returns in black ink as opposed to blue ink?
Can you help me move the sofa so I can retrieve the remote control that's slid underneath?	Can you tell me how the remote got there in the first place because I certainly didn't do it?
Can you call an ambulance for me?	Or do you think I can just get rid of this headache with Advil?

Worst of all, it sometimes works out that you're both having a bad week on the job at the same time. When that's the case, it's impossible to avoid the competitive instinct to see whose week sucks more:

Husband: Flenderson wants me to come in at six tomorrow morning so he can review the presentation before the meeting!

Wife: At least Flenderson is talking to you! Zuckerman was off getting a haircut while the rest of us worked through dinner.

Husband: At least you got dinner. Flenderson sends us home at 7:30 p.m. so the company doesn't have to pay for a meal.

Wife: You should have seen my dinner, though. It was some gross wrap sandwich. It gave me a stomachache.

Husband: Please. I'm still suffering from food poisoning after that lunch meeting Flenderson made me go to.

Wife: Yeah . . . well . . . Zuckerman hates rainbows. And smiles.

Husband: Ha! Flenderson was voted worst boss in North America by the readers of *Boss* magazine!

[*Husband and wife stare at each other for a few seconds in anger . . . and then run into the bedroom and have sex.*]

FAMILY BUSINESS

The battle between work and marriage has one easy solution: working at the same company. As you can imagine, the perks of this scenario are endless. As are the drawbacks.

Working at the Same Company as Your Spouse: Pros and Cons

Pro	Con
You get to save gas money by commuting together.	Ninety-seven percent of workdays begin with a disagreement about where to park.
You get to have lunch with the person you love . . .	. . . while listening to your coworkers constantly ask if you guys have ever made out in the office supply room.
You're instantly available to offer words of encouragement if your spouse is having an annoying day at the office.	Unless one of you is the person who's causing the annoying day.
You can be teammates on the company softball team.	When you strike out with the bases loaded to end the game, your spouse e-mails everyone and promises he or she is going to make sure you work on the fundamentals this off-season.
You can whisper sweet nothings in each other's ears when no one is looking.	Someone is, in fact, looking, and now it's kind of awkward that you've called your spouse "the Snuggle Master" in front of your colleagues.

An even more dramatic alternative than working at the same company is to go into business just the two of you. Many of the best and most successful small businesses in America are run by husband and wife teams, including:

- Restaurants
- Country inns
- Organized crime syndicates

When you run a business together, you don't have to worry about seeing each other enough. Instead, you have to worry about the opposite: when the hell will you get to spend any time apart? You'll both be working eighteen-hour days together to ensure that your business gets off the ground. Thus, a trip to the bathroom isn't so much a biological necessity as it is a chance to be alone for thirty seconds. As a result, you go to the bathroom seventeen times an hour.

For the Husband

Guys, do not use work as an excuse to avoid something you don't want to do with your spouse. In an earlier chapter, I encouraged wives not to blame a money issue if it's really something else that's bothering them. Now it's time for you, the husband, to come clean as well.

If you really have to work late, fine. But if you're just saying you have to work late so you can avoid having to hang out with your wife's family while they're in town, you're really asking for trouble.

Besides, if you're sitting in your office with nothing to do, your boss won't be impressed. He'll just think you're weird.

For the Wife

Ladies, as you're probably aware, there can sometimes be a lot of societal pressure for you to be a great wife, mother, and career woman all at the same time. Naturally, there are many moments when it's simply impossible to play all three roles simultaneously.

Here's the good news: your husband will understand. If your career is important to you, then it's important to your husband as well. So having to reschedule dinner plans because of a business trip doesn't suddenly make you a bad wife, even if it's something your grandmother insists she wouldn't have done back in her day. Don't worry about how other people used to balance their career and their marriage. You and your husband can do whatever works best for the two of you.

And if your grandmother continues to nag you, remind her that back in her day people also put asbestos in their walls and smoked when they were pregnant.

20
How Long Have We Been Married?

Celebrating Your Anniversaries

Every anniversary is special, but the first anniversary winds up being one of the most memorable. You're celebrating the end of your first year of marriage, which is an exciting achievement.

The first anniversary is the paper anniversary. Society came up with this tradition because you're still in massive debt from the wedding, so paper seems like something you can both afford. Plus, it sounds nicer than the "dirt" anniversary.

The paper anniversary represents one final step before the two of you can abandon the title of newlyweds. You have been learning to live together as husband and wife for 364 days. Before you graduate, though, there's a final exam. And, as so often seems to be the case, there are slightly different questions for the husband and the wife.

Final Exam for Wives

Pick out the best answer to each question. Don't worry. Even if you get a bunch of questions wrong, you'll still probably score higher than your husband will on his exam.

1. You want to give your husband personalized stationery as a paper anniversary gift. What sort of input should you get from him?

a. Does he want his middle name on the stationery?
b. Does he prefer full sheets of paper or note cards?
c. Does he prefer navy, gray, or black ink?
d. Does his opinion really matter?

2. What will be your husband's reaction when he gets the stationery?

a. "Oh, yes! *Yes!!!*"
b. "Guess you took that paper anniversary thing literally."
c. "It's definitely something I don't already have. So that's good. Right?"
d. "No new TV, huh?"

3. How many pieces of the personalized stationery will your husband use?

a. Two.
b. Seven.
c. Um, he can't find where he put it.
d. Do paper airplanes count as "using" it?

4. Will the gift of stationery give your husband the subtle hint that he should write more thank-you notes?

a. No.
b. The opposite of yes.
c. Absolutely not.
d. There will be no subtle hint taken on his end.

5. Your husband's birthday is only a couple of weeks after your anniversary. What would he like for his birthday?

a. Serving platters in your wedding china pattern.
b. New pillow shams because the old ones are looking a little threadbare.

c. Lavender soap.
d. Okay, these are really things that you want for your birthday, but your husband's getting the pillow shams anyway.

Okay, husbands, you're up:

Final Exam for Husbands

Pick the best answer to each question. You are allowed to cheat and talk to your male friends who have been married over a year, because even they don't know the right answer.

1. What present do I get my wife for our paper anniversary?

   a. Fancy stationery.
   b. A subscription to *USA Today*.
   c. Five hundred sheets of three-hole-punch paper.
   d. Diamond earrings.

2. Diamond earrings? What do they have to do with paper?

   a. Nothing.

3. Oh. I see. But I guess it doesn't really matter that they have nothing to do with paper because they're diamond earrings, right?

   a. Bingo.

4. Thanks.

   a. No problem.

5. So, after all that, how are you now going to justify getting your wife the subscription to *USA Today* instead of diamonds?

a. Everyone loves the color-coded sections!
b. I wanted to keep our insurance rates low.
c. Diamonds are forever, and since I already gave you one when we got engaged, I guess you're all set for life, huh?
d. At least I remembered to give you a gift. Remember what happened on your birthday?

Thinking Outside the (Paper) Box

The reality is that most couples don't feel the need to stick to the paper theme when it comes to giving a first anniversary gift, mostly because the wife already spent $1,200 on new stationery right after the wedding because she changed her name and couldn't very well be writing notes on cards that said Deborah Wainwright when her name was now Deborah Wainwright-Jacobson. I mean, how déclassé can you get?

Here are some other popular anniversary gift ideas for a husband to get his wife.

Flowers

Every woman loves getting a giant bouquet of flowers. They're romantic, they smell lovely, and they give you a chance to display one of the pretty vases you got as a wedding present. On the flip side, it's sort of unromantic when you say, "Ed got me an anniversary present, but it died two days later."

Jewelry

You don't actually have to get her diamond earrings. However, when she opens the gift, you want to say something like, "Honey, it's not diamond earrings, but it's almost as good. It's ______!" For the record, do not fill in the blank with any of the following:

- A candy bracelet!
- A mood ring!
- A stud for your tongue!
- Something I stole out of your jewelry box and rewrapped!
- Veal!

Leftover Registry Gifts

Your wife has been dying to get the twelfth teacup and saucer for a whole year, even though you've never used more than four teacups and saucers at any one point in time.

Something Sentimental

This is a sweet idea, but the only sentimental thing you can think of is to frame a nice photo of the two of you from the wedding. However, your wife has already done that with sixty-two other photos, and, frankly, she'd rather have the teacup and saucer.

Now, here are some popular choices for the wife to give the husband.

A Nice Watch

This is sort of the equivalent gift to him getting you nice jewelry. And since he's not doing that . . .

A New Flat-Screen TV

Good news: he'll love it. Bad news: all conversation between the two of you grinds to a halt for the next six months while he plays with the new toy.

Teacups and Saucers off Your Wedding Registry

Sure, he may hate it, but guess what: they're specially ordered from England and can't be returned. Ha!

A Deep-Fat Fryer for the Home

Now we're talking, sweetie!

Once the gifts have been exchanged and awkwardly complimented ("Now we have another framed photo of the two of us. How . . . consistent!") it's time to decide how you'll celebrate the actual anniversary day.

At first, you'll think about going away somewhere. What's more relaxing than a few days on the beach or in the mountains? But then you remember that you already took a romantic weekend trip away a few months ago and you're still trying to resolve the argument you've been having about whether or not breakfast was supposed to be included in the room rate.

Wife: I still can't believe we paid twenty-two dollars for a shiitake mushroom omelet!
Husband: I thought breakfast was included.
Wife: It wasn't!

A far simpler activity—but one that's just as romantic—is to return to the location where you got engaged. So you go to the bench down at the seashore where you popped the question . . . and notice that another couple is sitting on the bench, getting engaged. You're very happy for them, but they're certainly taking their sweet time, aren't they?

After you've watched this couple make out for about thirty-five minutes you notice that they start to take off their clothes. They begin to have sex on your bench. You run away, disgusted, and never return to the bench again.

Luckily, there's another sentimental spot you can return to: the site of your first date. You call Gino's Italian Café to make a reservation and learn that it's under new management. You figure that won't be much of a problem until you show up and realize that the new management is British Petroleum and that Gino's is now an oil refinery. The workers claim that there's an on-site commissary you can visit, but you decline because British food sucks.

So, the two of you return home, light some candles, crack open a bottle of champagne, and have the most romantic night imaginable . . . until the candles get knocked over and set the rug on fire.

Unfinished Business

The first anniversary is, of course, a major milestone. It's been one whole year since your wedding. Remember your wedding? Of course you do. But you still flip through the wedding album and watch the DVD while pretending you haven't already done this 291 times. The reason you do this, though, is because the first anniversary reminds you that it's time to settle your unfinished wedding business.

When you watch the DVD you remember that the videographer was supposed to send you extra copies for you to give to your parents. That, of course, never happened. And now, like that final sequence in *The Godfather*, it's time for you to settle any outstanding family business. So while you and your spouse attend the baptism of Connie's baby, you send Clemenza and Al Neri out to tie up loose ends.

Unfinished Wedding Business
That Needs to Be Settled Before the First Anniversary

1. Unused serving platter finally returned to Macy's for store credit (which, in turn, is never used).

2. Framed photo of you having your first dance together finally sent to your parents who, by now, have no memory of the event whatsoever.

3. Photo proofs that you were supposed to put into an album are instead stuffed into a shoebox, thrown in the closet, and ignored for the rest of time.

4. Bride's dress sent to the dry cleaner's to be hermetically sealed. It will be reopened in twenty-five years so that your daughter can laugh at it and break your heart.

5. Groom's rented tux finally returned to a store with a name like Tux to Be You. With late fee, the tux now costs more than the bride's dress.

6. Last bunch of wedding RSVP cards from your guests finally arrive in the mail.

Future Anniversaries

The first anniversary isn't the only one with a gift-giving theme.

Year 2: The Cotton Anniversary

After the complications of paper, you're thrown a bone in year two. Cotton means clothing, which couldn't be simpler, right?

Well . . . the wife decides that it's time to expand the husband's drab wardrobe, so she picks out a new outfit that the husband doesn't like and never wears.

The husband, meanwhile, isn't comfortable buying women's clothing, so he goes for a raincoat, which is nice, and also contains zero cotton.

Year 3: Leather

Wife gives husband an amazing leather coat. Husband gives wife a sexy Catwoman outfit (with leather whip). Wife returns Catwoman outfit and, as punishment, keeps leather jacket for herself.

Year 4: Flowers

Husband gets his wife the most beautiful bouquet of all time. And while she's enjoying the gift, this conversation takes place:

Wife: These are beautiful, sweetie!

Husband: I'm so glad you like them. Hey . . . did you ever take back that Catwoman outfit I gave you last year?

Wife:	I tried to, but they would only give me a store credit, and there was nothing else I wanted at that crazy store.
Husband:	So you still have the outfit?
Wife:	Somewhere.
Husband:	Do you . . .
Wife:	No.
Husband:	Just for a few . . .
Wife:	No.
Husband:	I could . . .
Wife:	No.

Year 5: Wood

By now, the wife is really in the mood for jewelry, but she feels bad asking for that as a gift. And then the husband makes yet another remark about the Catwoman suit, and suddenly the guilt is gone.

Year 6 and Onward

It's completely impossible to remember what the gift tie-in is for all these anniversaries. In fact, it's an accomplishment simply to remember that you *have* an anniversary. So you nickname each anniversary the "memory anniversary" and spend the whole day talking about how lucky you are to be married to (can someone please remind me of the name of my spouse?).

For the Husband and for the Wife

You've both earned some congratulations. You've successfully kept the love alive for the first few years of marriage. It's an impressive achievement and you should be proud.

And, as a result, the two of you now know that you can accomplish anything together . . . except maybe agree on the fastest way to the airport.

Spouse: Sweetie, why do you insist on taking Elm Street to the airport?
You: It has less traffic than Ocean Avenue.
Spouse: [*laughing*] How many times have we had this conversation?
You: [*also laughing*] At least once a year for our whole marriage!
Spouse: I know, right! Like at least six times!
You: Seven.
Spouse: Huh?
You: We've been married for seven years.
Spouse: We have?

21
Signs You May Actually Be in Trouble

As I said in the introduction, the goal of this book is to discuss marriage growing pains that are normal and healthy. But sadly for some folks, the bumps in the first year of marriage cause their "relationship car" to lose control and swerve off the road. And then burst into flames.

Which leads to the following concern: do you have good car insurance? Just kidding. (You don't.) No, the question is: are you having normal marital issues or are you moving into the annulment zone?

Here are some of the warning signs.

Cohabitation Warning Sign

Normal Marital Issue:	Wife complains that husband is being too messy around the house.
Annulment Zone:	Wife takes husband's possessions and burns them in the backyard during druidlike ceremony.

Parental Warning Sign

Normal Marital Issue:	Wife wants to have kids right away, but husband wants to wait . . .
Annulment Zone:	. . . because he has so many other kids living all over the country.

Sexual Warning Sign

Normal Marital Issue:	Husband gets aroused while watching a movie starring Jessica Alba.
Annulment Zone:	Husband can get aroused *only* while watching a movie starring Jessica Alba.

Emotional Warning Sign

Normal Marital Issue:	When wife arrives home from work, she seems as excited to read *People* magazine as she is to greet her husband.
Annulment Zone:	If *People* magazine hasn't arrived, wife bursts into tears and shouts, "That is the only good thing in my miserable life!"

Financial Warning Sign

Normal Marital Issue:	Wife is upset with amount of money husband spent on new stereo.
Annulment Zone:	Wife is upset with amount of money husband spent on new mistress.

Social Warning Sign

Normal Marital Issue:	Wife wants to socialize more than husband.
Annulment Zone:	Husband agrees to socialize more, as long as he can dress up as a British spy named Nigel and take urgent phone calls from MI6 during dinner.

Vacation Warning Sign

Normal Marital Issue:	During romantic weekend away, wife complains too much about the poor service at the hotel.
Annulment Zone:	Wife picks fight with concierge, and then challenges him to a duel.

Job-Related Warning Sign

Normal Marital Issue:	Husband bails on social plans at the last minute because he has to work late.
Annulment Zone:	Husband sleeps at the office because "the fax machine is the only one who understands me."

If annulment seems too extreme, you can always take the more traditional route:

1. Go to couples counseling.
2. Agree that it's working.
3. Each have an affair.
4. Cover up the affair.

5. Halfheartedly deny the affair after it's exposed.
6. Go back to couples counseling.
7. Blame the therapist.
8. Get new therapist.
9. Make love.

If you want more information on this method, at least one of your aunts or uncles will have tried it out, so you can just ask them.

22

The Road to Twenty-five

The twenty-fifth anniversary will be here before you know it! Seriously—when it arrives, you really *won't know it*, because you'll be busy trying to figure out where you put your blood pressure medication.

The good news is that once you get through the first few years and reach your marriage cruising altitude, the journey to twenty-five promises to be a smooth flight. Here are some expected highlights.

Year Six

Small and moving ceremony held in husband's closet when the final piece of his wedding tux is discovered to be lost / destroyed / 532 percent too small.

Year Nine

You both decide that the moment is right to redo the master bathroom because you each want your own sink. In fact, having a large master bathroom has become so important that you'll gladly borrow space from other rooms, like the dining room (you can eat in the hallway).

Year Ten

The two of you buy your first really expensive piece of art . . . and hang it upside down.

Year Twelve

Small and moving ceremony held to commemorate the moment when the husband officially has more hair on his ears than on his scalp.

Year Thirteen

The whole family gets to go live in a hotel for a week after the husband tries to fix a small plumbing problem in the kitchen.

Year Fifteen

Highlights of family vacation to Florida:

- Sunburn (husband)
- Allergies (wife)
- Hatred of everyone (daughter)
- Dangerous obsession with sharks (son)
- Constant concern about where you're having the next meal (grandparents)

Year Seventeen

Small and moving ceremony held to commemorate death of household pet, which you got after repeated pleas from your children, who then played with the pet for seven minutes and never looked at it again. In fact, the children wanted to attend the small and moving ceremony for the pet, but they were out doing "stuff."

Year Nineteen

You accidentally celebrate your twentieth anniversary this year.

Year Twenty-two

The two of you take a romantic vacation to France. You have such a great time that you call the children and tell them you're never coming home. Your daughter picks up the phone and says that's cool. However, she's clearly having a house party in the background, so you promptly fly home and find that the Scotch in your bar now tastes remarkably like iced tea.

Year Twenty-four

Friend of the wife's leaves her husband and runs off to live in Tuscany with some handsome Italian winemaker. Husband promptly buys wife some flowers. Every day. For the rest of time.

Year Twenty-five

The silver anniversary! The two of you decide to take out your wedding album and flip through it . . . only to remember that you lost it seventeen years ago when it was accidentally recycled along with some old issues of *National Geographic*. Now you know why yellow is not a popular color for wedding albums.

Conclusion

Nothing Is More Fun than Being Married

Okay. So the first few years of marriage may have been a little different from what you expected. You've bounced some checks, disagreed about the optimal TV volume, and had a shocking number of debates about what brand of toilet paper is fluffiest.

And yet, it's truly the most wonderful time in your life because:

1. You are in love.
2. You *don't* have to plan a wedding.

Those two factors alone are the most powerful combination since the peanut met the M&M.

But there's an added bonus as well: during the first year of marriage you get to continually celebrate the fact that you are no longer twenty-two and single.

For years, society has lied to recent college grads and told them that they are about to enter the best time in their lives. As you grow older, though, you quickly realize that this was just something that colleges tell their seniors so that they'll go away and make room for new students. But once you realize that the real world doesn't come with a meal plan, it's too late. Some eighteen-year-old jackass is sleeping in your dorm room and drinking your beer.

During the bumps in the road of marriage, there may be a brief moment when you think that the grass was greener back when you were twenty-two and single. So you take out an old photo album and remember that the grass was not greener—in fact, it was brown and spewing methane gas.

Bump in the Road During First Year of Marriage	Corresponding Bump in the Road from When You Were Twenty-two and Single
The two of you can't agree where to have dinner and you wind up at a restaurant neither of you loves.	When you go out to dinner, it's always for someone's massive twenty-third birthday party; you sit at the table for six hours and manage to be served only a roll and some ketchup.
Your romantic weekend plans are canceled because one of you has to work.	Your romantic weekend plans are canceled because your Internet date wound up being a fugitive.
Some random relative of your spouse is coming to stay with you for a week.	Some random friend from college is crashing with you "just for a while." Also this person needs to borrow your bed three times a week for sex.
You buy a new refrigerator and immediately realize you can't afford it.	You buy a carton of milk and immediately realize you can't afford it.

Thus, as you both reflect back on your first years of marriage, you'll realize how truly fortunate and lucky you are to have each other.

Every couple will tell you that the words they exchanged on their wedding day are even more meaningful years later:

Words Exchanged on Wedding Day: "We're soul mates."
Assessment Years Later: Still true.

Words Exchanged on Wedding Day: "As long as we're together, the bad times will be easier and the good times will be that much better."
Assessment Years Later: Absolutely.

Words Exchanged on Wedding Day: "Who the hell is that random guy in the first row?"
Assessment Years Later: Seriously—he's in all the pictures! Did we ever find out who the hell he was?

These words from your wedding day will only continue to magnify in significance as the years go by, which means that the best times are still ahead. Enjoy them. You're going to have a great life together.

And if anyone knows the name of that random guy who was in the first row at my wedding, can you let me know?